MIRACLES
Every Day

WHEN MIRACLES HAPPEN
True Stories of God's Divine Touch

Edited by Mary Hollingsworth

Guideposts Books
Carmel, New York

Acknowledgments

Every attempt has been made to credit the sources of copyrighted material used in this book. If any such acknowledgment has been inadvertently omitted or miscredited, receipt of such information would be appreciated.

All material that originally appeared in Guideposts publicatons is reprinted with permission. Copyright © Guideposts, Carmel, NY.

Unless otherwise noted, Scripture quotations are taken from *The Holy Bible*, New International Version. Copyright © 1973, 1978, 1984, International Bible Society. Used by permission of Zondervan Bible Publishers. Scripture quotations marked NCV are taken from *The Holy Bible*, New Century Version®, copyright © 1987, 1988, 1991 by Thomas Nelson, Inc. Used by permission. Scripture quotations marked KJV are from the King James Version.

"The First Day", "A Lesson in Childlike Faith", and "Prayer Boots" published by permission from *Whispers from Heaven*, copyright © Publications International, Ltd. "Discovering the Real Miracles" by Norris Burkes. Syndicated columnist with Gannett News Service. www.thechaplain.net; "She Gave the Softest Hugs" excerpted from *In the Company of Women* ©1994 by Brenda Hunter, Ph.D. Used by permission of WaterBrook Multnomah Publishing Group, a division of Random House, Inc.; "If You're Willing to Ask" by Andrea Peterson excerpted from *Mom, You Make a Difference* by Elisa Morgan. Grand Rapids, MI: Fleming H. Revell, a division of Baker Book House, 2005.

"Surprise! It's God" by Kathryn Lay, "Nothing's Too Small for God" by Gail McWilliams, "A Walk on the Beach" by Nancy B. Gibbs, "Amazing Love" by Greg Asimakoupoulos, "Always on Time" by Rhonda Brown, "Be Still" by Elizabeth Schmeidler, "A Meal for a Miracle" by Sue Ferguson, "Lost in the Fire" and "Caught in the Jackknife" by Mary Hollingsworth, "We Believe in Miracles and CPR" and "Getting Out of God's Way" by Barbara Curtis, "Comfort Zone" by Faith Gray, "Everyday Miracles" by Donna Lowich, "Are We There Yet?" by Joanne K. Hill, "Through Rain and Hail" by Peggy Frezon, "A Burgundy Valentine" by Donna Arlynn Frisinger, "A Kiss from My Heavenly Daddy" and "Relaxing in His Love" by Holly Baxley, "The Crumpled Yellow Note" by Vicki P. Graham, "The Ultimate Realtor" by Pamela R. Watts, "Snow Angel" by Stephanie Terry, "A Love of a Lifetime" by Austin-Nichole Zachrich, "Bloom Where Planted" by Peggy Frezon, "Out of the Mouths of Babes" by Pam Frantz, "The Miracle of the Sofa" by Zarette Beard, "What If?" by Marsha Jordan, "On to Africa" by Melody Rain; are used by permission of the authors.

Editorial, research, and content development managed by Shady Oaks Studio, Bedford, Texas. Team members: Patty Crowley, Vicki Graham, Rhonda Hogan, Mary Hollingsworth, Mary Kay Knox, Kathryn Murray, Nancy Sullivan, Stephanie Terry, and Barbara Tork.

www.guideposts.org
(800) 431-2344
Guideposts Books & Inspirational Media Division

Illustrations by Ron Bucalo
Cover design by The DesignWorks Group, Inc.
Cover photo by Shutterstock

Printed in the United States of America

Contents

*C*HAPTER 2   BEFORE YOU EVEN ASK

*C*HAPTER 3   TOUCHES FROM HEAVEN

CHAPTER 4   WHEN YOU LEAST EXPECT IT

CHAPTER 5 DAY BY DAY WITH GOD

Introduction

When something remarkable happens in our everyday lives, we have all kinds of names for it. We call it "coincidence." We call it an "accident." We call it "mysterious." We call it "fate." In fact, we call it everything but what it really is—we rarely call it a "miracle from God."

And yet, how else can you explain the unexplainable? How can you brush away the unbelievable? How can you solve the supernatural puzzles of life? If God is not the answer, how do you cope with the mysterious happenings in your life?

Whether we call it by the right name or not, and whether we understand it or not, God *is* the answer—the only answer we need. And when we begin to recognize God's presence in miracles that happen every day and call them by the right name, we find great comfort and joy.

In *Miracles Every Day*, you will see God in action in the lives of ordinary people just like you. And, perhaps, you will begin to grasp the undeniable fact that He is working in your life too.

In Chapter 1, "Small Surprises," you'll see how Kathryn's losing her hair during chemotherapy gives her a new joy. Carol finds out that nothing is too small for God to care about. And Therese learns a lesson in child-like faith from her three-year-old daughter at a baseball game.

God answers prayers Before You Even Ask, in Chapter 2 as Rhonda discovers when an EMT shows up at just the right moment without having been called. Meanwhile Joanne experiences God's constant protection when she runs out of gas on a lonely mountain road. And Sue receives a miracle in return for a meal she prepares for friends, even when she couldn't afford to do it.

The stories in Chapter 3, "Touches from Heaven," reveal God's vigilance in our lives, such as sending Donna a burgundy valentine. Peggy learns that God is always there for her, even through rain and hail. And Pamela is astonished to meet the Ultimate Realtor in the nick of time.

God often comes into your life When You Least Expect It, as Chapter 4 demonstrates. Mary feels God's presence when she is caught in a jackknife. Austin celebrates a love of a lifetime. And Stephanie meets a snow angel in the middle of a blizzard.

In Chapter 5, "Day by Day with God," Barbara learns that the best way to solve life's puzzles is by getting out of God's way. Andrea discovers that miracles really do happen if you're willing to ask for them. And Elizabeth comes to love God more because of her bout with yellow fever.

Each of these true stories will shine a divine light on this truth: God is alive and well! He loves us with an overwhelming love. And He protects us, provides for us, and straightens our paths with miracles every day.

MARY HOLLINGSWORTH

MIRACLES
Every Day

CHAPTER 1

Small Surprises

Two sparrows cost only a penny, but not even one of them can die without your Father's knowing it. God even knows how many hairs are on your head. So don't be afraid. You are worth much more than many sparrows (Matthew 10:29–30 NCV).

We often think that the little things in our lives that trouble us day by day are not worth the attention of the Almighty. Surely He is more concerned with wars, governments, and international disasters than He is about the pain in my hand. And yet, His Word says that He even knows how many hairs are on our heads. Be assured—God is never too busy to be concerned about the details in our lives. It's there that He sends us small surprises of His love.

The Brightest Miracle

SHARI SMYTH

I n the spring my mare will have a foal. I pray that it will be born all right. But it is winter on our farm now and snow, like a crushed velvet blanket, covers the fields. The biting wind bows even the majestic evergreens that circle our house.

From the second floor of my weathered barn I listen to the wind rattle the tin roof like a toy and watch it sweep down over the slopes of the hills and shiver the stream that is almost frozen.

Below me, huddled inside the stone-walled paddock, are the horses. Puffs of cold, white breath escape from their mouths as they wait impatiently to be fed.

The calf is bawling and the pigs grunting hungrily. But for just a moment I pause to start my day off right. The barn is my sanctuary . . . my sacred ground . . . where God and I talk. He teaches me about life from the simple things around me.

Today I notice how dark and naked is the forest that borders my land with knobby branches stretching like bony fingers to the gray sky.

"So like you without Me," I hear Him say.

As I fill the metal grain buckets I think about all the life sleeping in the trunks of those trees and beneath the frozen ground. Waiting for the warmth—and for something else that no one has ever fully understood—to tell it to wake up and grow.

I remember the story my mother used to read to me that asks, "Who makes the wind to blow? Who makes the flowers to grow? Who makes us to grow? God does." So simple. And yet so profound that prickles rise on my skin as I carry the buckets down to my hungry horses.

They—a gray, a chestnut, and a dappled gray—are still inside the stone-walled paddock. When they see me their ears perk forward and then flatten back as they nudge each other out of the way to be first. Just like children.

Finally the boss horse trots into his stall triumphantly with a "You'd better feed me first" look. I do. Then the chestnut. Then my baby—a tiny, nine-hands-high Shetland. While pouring her grain into the manger I notice her stomach is beginning to thicken, and again I pray that her foal will be born all right.

The cold begins to get to me and I hurry to feed the cow and pigs. On my way I remember why the animals can stay out in the cold and not suffer. Every fall their coat begins to grow gradually, so there is no shock to the system. Finally, when winter hits in all her fury, they are safe inside a woolly rug of fur. In addition, the skin secretes a layer of waterproof oil as double protection.

Before I go in to the beckoning warmth, I thank my Creator for His faithfulness to all His creatures. I thank Him, too, for the dark beauty of winter dressed in her swirling white gown and jewels of crystal ice. And for spring that never fails to come. It teaches me something about the cold, dark times in my own life.

Finally, after months of waiting, I can smell the raw earth and feel the warm sun kiss my face and sink into my bones. The once cutting wind is now like silk against my cheek. Shiny green fingers of foliage are pushing up everywhere. The stream is dancing and singing over the rocks. Joining in the chorus are birds from every tree chirping silver-fluted notes to prospective mates. My senses reel as I remember how Jesus said God knows every bird.

My mare's stomach is very round and firm, like a ripe pear. Underneath she is ready to give milk to her foal. Her time will soon be here.

As I watch her trotting clumsily down to the stream, I think of the wonder of a life growing inside another life; of the start from an egg and a sperm—too small for the naked eye, but containing all the ingredients of a full-grown pony; of the wonder of everything born after its kind, as God said so long ago.

I wait. Nothing happens. From my barn I see the clusters of purple violets peeking out from the grass, so resilient to trampling feet. I hope my mare is as strong in giving birth.

"Be patient," my friend who knows about horses says. "It's been a hard winter and this is her first foal."

"I know. That's what I'm worried about."

Restlessly I sleep in my mare's stall, listening to the stream and the mournful wail of a train whistle. Still nothing. She is now two weeks late.

Bleary-eyed, I go out again the next night. As I struggle with the bailing twine, something stops me from throwing the hay down to my mare. Rushing to her stall, I shine my lantern over the gate. It is there, lying in wet straw. Just born.

I stand frozen as the mother licks off the transparent birth sack.

Carefully I open the gate and kneel in the straw. The foal struggles to stand on its long, spindly legs. Its downy-soft coat is a cinnamon color with a white star above the eyes. A suggestion of a mane covers the top of the neck. It is a filly. A girl. And she is healthy. I bow my head in thanks.

The filly nuzzles her mother with sucking noises looking for milk. How extraordinary, I think, that she is born knowing she must eat. And knowing the food is somewhere on her mother. I watch my new miracle and realize it happens every second all over the world.

Every day I am surrounded by miracles so ordinary I don't think about them. But tonight, flooded with love for my new filly, I do think about them.

They flash by me in a kaleidoscope of colors until I come to the brightest one of all. The miracle that caused God to become flesh two thousand years ago in a barn with cows, donkeys, and pigeons looking on. Perhaps a new foal was born in the same barn that night too. My mind can't comprehend His birth. But my soul glows with the beauty of it. The King of kings born in a barn!

Softly I move to the stall door. My foal has found one of the nipples and is sucking noisily. I can leave them alone now.

Outside the stars are brilliant in their bed of black sky. It is spring and God has given me a healthy foal. What more could I ask?

Surprise! It's God

KATHRYN LAY

S omeone mowed the lawn," my husband said as we
drove into the driveway.

I was in a lot of pain from my ride home from the
hospital, but I knew my husband and daughter had been
busy the last four days with me at the hospital and
weren't concerned with things like taking care of the
lawn.

It was to be the first of many ways God showed His
love through our friends as I recovered from a hysterec-
tomy and began months of chemo for uterine cancer.

Our family was scared of what lay ahead. Would the
chemo stop the cancer that had spread? How sick would
I be? Would I be able to do all the things I needed to do?
What did our future hold?

I could look back on many things in my life that truly
reflected God's love—our daughter's adoption, my husband's dream teaching job finally realized, a home of our
own after twenty years of marriage, my first children's
book sale.

But I never dreamed how much God would show us

His love in so many surprising ways during the most difficult time of our lives.

Two weeks after my first chemo treatment, my hair began to fall out. I couldn't believe how hard it was to have this happen. While in the waiting room for my next treatment, there were four women nearby, laughing and talking together. I glanced at the women wearing baseball caps, barely hiding their bald heads. I touched my head a moment.

The four women told stories of their individual hair loss situations. As they talked of how they lost their hair, joking over stories of adventures with wigs, hats, and scarves, I began to feel sick to my stomach. Suddenly, I began to cry quietly and couldn't stop. My husband reached over and took my hand.

I often felt well other than the first few days after chemo, but I knew with my hair loss that even when I felt good, I'd have that constant reminder of my illness. How could I escape the fear?

The next morning, I read the daily devotional that I received every morning in an email.

"LUKE 12:7 NIV, Indeed, the very hairs of your head are all numbered. Don't be afraid; you are worth more than many sparrows."

I thought of the hairs in my hairbrush, on my pillow, in my hat I was wearing. I reached up and ran my fingers through my hair and found more than a dozen strands had come loose.

The devotional comforted me when I realized that even though they weren't on my head anymore, God knew how many strands were in my brush, on my pillow, in my hat, and in my hand. He had counted them all. With or without the hair on my head, God knew me and what my future held.

A few days after most of my hair had gone, I received a check from a friend at church who had raised funds from other friends for me to order a wig and whatever other coverings I wanted to help me feel better. God's love was shown again through His children.

The wig was a hit. Everyone loved it. Family and friends praised how good it looked on me.

Did God number the hairs on my wig?

I was still afraid. Afraid of the cancer, the chemo, the upcoming CT scan and its results. But I knew God would be with me through it all.

And how could I not believe it when again and again God surprised me with small, but special gifts.

Our church had been extremely kind about making sure we had meals for three weeks after surgery and for the first four days after each chemo treatment when I was feeling so bad. One night, a woman from church I had only met once brought our family a meal. She asked if I needed anything the next day. I told her no, that my daughter would be in school all day, and I would probably just be sleeping off the pain medicine.

That next day, I slept all morning and woke up a few

minutes before noon, realizing how hungry I was, but feeling too weak to get up and cook something. I whispered, "I'm hungry God."

A few moments later, the doorbell rang. I put on my hat and looked through the window. Standing at the door was the woman from the night before. When I opened the door she said, "I won't come in, but I was just coming back from prayer at church and thought you might be able to use this."

She held out a sack with a burger and shake in it. Like an angel, she smiled and left. I was amazed. God had answered my prayer before I voiced it, while I still slept. If she'd have come earlier, I'd have been asleep and might not have heard the door. If she'd have been much later, I might have struggled to the kitchen to find something to eat. It wasn't a parting of the Red Sea, but I knew this was a miracle.

Nearly halfway into my treatments, my husband and I planned an overnight trip. We needed the time alone, to be a couple, to relax from all the stress and think about only us, not the cancer, the bills, the treatments. Friends invited our daughter to spend the night and on Friday, I packed and got ready for our little trip an hour away to a pretty little hotel on a lake in a town full of antique shops in a charming square we'd always loved.

Money was tight and we were only able to go because of a royalty check I'd received weeks ago. As I got everything ready for us to leave straight from picking my husband up at work, I thought about how nice it would be to have a little extra money so we wouldn't have to be so strict on our meals.

It was 4:00 P.M. and I had to leave in twenty minutes to pick up my husband. The mail was unusually late, but when it came, I was surprised to receive an acceptance of an essay I'd written for a magazine that paid when the piece was published. Inside the envelope with the copy of the magazine and a letter of congratulations with fifty dollars in cash.

It was the first time I'd submitted anything to this magazine, but of the hundreds of writing sales I'd made before, I'd never had anyone send cash. I was glad though, as I didn't time to go across town to our bank and still pick my husband up in time.

After our return from our wonderfully restful trip, I mentioned to a friend about the surprise acceptance. She'd written many times for this publication. She said, "That's a miracle, Kathy. I've always received a check from them."

Since that time, I've had other acceptances from them and it was always a check. There was no explanation from them for the cash payment, but I know it was God working to show me again how much He loved me, in spite of this terrifying time in my life.

I've been given good medical reports recently and changed from chemo to medication, sooner than the doctor expected. I know that whatever happens in the weeks and months to come, God loves me the same as He always has.

I've always loved surprises. But now, I am able to share with many around me how God has used others in my life to surprise me over and over, each surprise a giant card from God that says, "I love you, Kathy."

Prayer Boots

CAROL STIGGER

Amy, my teenage daughter, was too busy getting ready for school to eat breakfast sitting down, so I delivered a glass of juice to her room. Her algebra book was propped against a mirror, and she was reading it while braiding her hair.

"I know you're worried about your test," I said. "Just remember that God cares about the little details of our lives along with the big ones."

The mirror reflected Amy's frown. "With water pollution and nuclear proliferation, drug wars and global warming to deal with, I seriously doubt that my algebra quiz is a big priority with God."

"But you are a priority with God," I said.

Amy drank her juice and handed me the empty glass. "Thirty-five thousand children die every day of starvation. Shouldn't I pray for them instead of for my quiz?"

How could I explain the heart of God to my big-hearted daughter? On my drive to work, I wanted to talk that little problem over with God, but I was too concerned at the moment about Amy going to school in

thin-soled, scuffed, teen-approved footwear. I did not
know what to call them and had failed to talk her out of
them. The boots I had bought her the day before were
warm, skid-proof, flat, and knee high. She said they
looked like old-lady boots and refused to wear them.
Knowing there was no chance of winning the argument,
I finally told her I'd return them to the store on my way
home. Amy's rejected boots sat on the seat beside me as
I drove to work, and I was annoyed that one more chore
had been added to my day.

Snow was falling faster than my windshield wipers
could erase it. A car in front of me slid into the ditch. I
prayed that God would keep me and the other travelers
safe. The fact that my daughter cared more about fashion than frostbite suddenly seemed less important than
the dangerous highways. I was pleased that Amy was
concerned about starving children, but how could I
explain that God is always listening, always cares, no
matter how small the detail? I knew that God was steering my car, keeping me from skidding out of control, but
that was a big detail. No time to ask God for answers this
morning, just a quick prayer of gratitude once I arrived
safely at work.

My staff spent most of the morning finding excuses to
go to the supply room so they could watch the snowdrifts
accumulate outside the windows. By early afternoon, an
ice storm was breaking tree limbs. Everyone cheered when

I read the memo that said our office was closing early so we could get home safely. Nancy, an elderly woman on my staff, looked so frightened that I delayed my quick exit in order to talk with her.

She pointed to her shoes. They looked new and matched her blue skirt. Even her earrings looked specially chosen to complement the shoes. They were the first shoes with a little heel she had worn since her hip surgery. She said she had been too excited about being fashionable again to heed the weather report. Now the sidewalks were covered with ice. She was afraid she would fall and re-injure her hip.

I offered to drive her to the bus stop. She clung tightly to my arm across the parking lot, but I wondered how she would manage the six-block walk from the bus to her apartment. I opened the car door for her, and there were those boots: warm, skid-proof, flat, knee high—and just her size.

"Thank God!" she exclaimed.

I squeezed her hand. "And Amy," I added.

When I got home, Amy was warming her feet on the radiator. "You were right about those boots, Mom," she said.

"And so were you, dear."

She looked surprised.

"Your boots were the answer to a little prayer." I told her about Nancy.

She looked astonished and then chagrined. "My little prayer was that my algebra test would be postponed until tomorrow so I would have more time to study. Then the weather got so bad they sent us home."

This conversation was going in the wrong direction, like too many of our conversations lately. "I hope you don't think your prayer caused the ice storm!" I exclaimed.

"No . . . I'm just amazed that with all the prayers going up to God about tests and weather and saving the whales and world peace and famines, He had time to give boots I did not want to someone who needed them."

I nodded, relieved that she was understanding more than I had supposed.

"Mom, did you say the boots were her exact size?"

I nodded again.

"That is such a little detail. I mean, they would have worked if they were too big or just a size too small."

"But don't you think Nancy felt more loved, more cared for, to find that the boots were a perfect fit?"

"Well, if you bought me boots that pinched my feet, I would think you were merely doing your duty."

I knew I did not have to explain this any further, but I said, "Love is in the details." I felt like I had just learned this again myself.

Nothing's Too Small for God

GAIL McWILLIAMS

My name is Gail McWilliams. I'm seventy-three years old and fought every step of the way not to succumb to the ailments of aging. I finally agreed to cataract surgery, and that was a miracle in itself! But that was it, I told myself.

Then one day I realized I was missing out on my friends' conversations; I couldn't hear the preacher, and I was beginning to think people were whispering behind my back. I finally broke down and went to a hearing specialist where I learned I had lost the majority of my hearing, and I was a prime candidate for a pair of those new digital hearing aids.

At the urging of friends I invested in the digital devices, learned how to insert them, and how to keep them charged. Wonder of wonders, I could hear again! I was part of the crowd again, and it felt good.

Alas, one night after my shower, I realized I had

inserted them into the wrong ears. As I worked to pull one from my ear, I dropped it, and it rolled out of sight. Frantic, I scrambled around on my hands and knees, but I found no tiny device. I was in tears.

As is my habit when I need help from God, I called a friend and she prayed with me, not only that I would find the aid but that God would help me get them in the correct ears. In my unfaithfulness I told God it would be enough just to find the instrument, and then I'd resume my struggles to apply them in the correct canals.

Never limit God! I searched and prayed, and prayed and searched, but to no avail. I gave up and went to the bathroom for a pity party. On my way I suddenly realized the muffled static that had been all I could hear from my television was now clear and loud. Could it be?

I stood at the bathroom mirror holding my hand mirror so I could see my ears. All by myself, I gave a huge shout of "Glory!" There in each ear was a perfectly and correctly placed digital hearing aid. God had not only located my missing digital, but He had kindly removed the first one to the right ear and then lovingly found the missing one and placed it in the correct ear.

Don't limit what He wants to do for you. Nothing is too small!

It Wasn't My Fault, Mama!

MARION BOND WEST

It wasn't my fault," Jon, one of our ten-year-old twin sons, wailed as I loudly accused him of spilling Kool-Aid in front of the refrigerator.

I sighed in silent anger. It seemed that nothing had ever been Jon's fault. Even when he was a little fellow and could hardly talk, he'd shake his head and insist, "No, not me." I knew I could make him wipe up the spilled drink, but we couldn't really communicate about it. Just as I expected, he grumbled and wiped it up and went away mad. I was angry too.

While Jon and I seemed to go in circles about his always insisting he was innocent, Jon and his daddy almost never disagreed. It often seemed to me that Jerry, my husband, wasn't stern enough with the boys, especially Jon.

Jon adored his daddy and was always right on his heels, watching him shave, talking a mile a minute, or following him around the house.

One Saturday morning Jerry planned to trim limbs

on the oak tree in our back yard. Jon, of course, was helping his daddy. Jeremy had gone down the street to play with friends.

In about an hour Jerry came in the back door. He slammed it so hard that I knew right away something was wrong. Jon followed without comment.

"What's the matter?" I asked.

"I did a stupid thing. Fell off the ladder. I don't know how it happened, but I seem to have done something to my arm. Can't move it."

Jerry's almost never sick or hurt, so I figured he'd soon be fine. And I was surprised when he said, "You'd better take me to the emergency room."

Jon asked to go and I said he could, leaving our sixteen-year-old, Jennifer, in charge of Jeremy. At the emergency room, we had a long wait. Jon sat close to his daddy and was unusually quiet and well-behaved. Finally, Jerry was X-rayed and a doctor reported the results. "The large bone in your upper arm is broken, about three inches below the shoulder. It's a bad break."

Jon and I were silent in amazement. Jerry was always fine!

The doctor continued, "No work for a couple of weeks. Don't get in the tub, don't drive. Move as little as possible. You'll need a hospital bed because you'll have to sleep sitting up."

We left the emergency room with Jerry in a wheelchair,

his shirt draped over his shoulder, the empty sleeve dangling by his side. They had set the arm, and it was strapped to his body.

"I'll go get the car, Jon. You stay with Daddy." Jon nodded and placed one hand on his daddy's good left arm.

Riding home, Jon sat between us, saying almost nothing. But he kept looking at Jerry's empty shirt sleeve.

Back at the house it was almost dark. The cut limbs and overturned ladder were still in the backyard. From the kitchen window I watched Jon walking around where the accident had happened. He tugged at a limb still connected by bark to the large oak tree. It wouldn't come off, so he let it go. He set the ladder up and stood looking at the tree for quite a while. I called him for his bath. He came, still looking over his shoulder at the tree.

As we got ready for bed Jon came and stood looking at his daddy sitting up in the hospital bed. "Can you sleep in that thing, Daddy?" he asked, running his hand over the foot of the metal bed.

"Yeah, I'll get used to it, son. You go on to bed. 'Night."

Jerry slept well. The next morning, Jennifer came into the kitchen. "Mama, I have to talk to you," she said.

"Jon came into my room last night. I woke up real late and he was just standing there in the moonlight. You and Daddy were asleep. He looked real scared. You know how nothing is ever Jon's fault? Well, you won't believe what he told me. He said, 'Jen, it was all my fault. The whole thing.' Then he explained that he had pulled at a limb while Daddy was on the ladder, not knowing that it was still connected to the tree. When he couldn't get it off, he simply turned it loose. It snapped back like a slingshot and turned the ladder over. Remember how Daddy kept saying the ladder seemed to have been knocked right out from under him?"

"Oh, Jen, I never suspected. Jon's been quiet, but I didn't know this. I'll have to tell Daddy."

When Jerry came downstairs I told him. A silent pain shot through his eyes—much more pain than when he'd broken his arm. After breakfast everyone had left the table except Jon and Jerry. I was at the sink, thinking how I'd start with a lecture.

Jerry spoke, "Jon, Jennifer told us what you told her last night. She had to, son. We needed to know." Jerry's voice was so gentle, I turned to look at him. The grave expression on Jon's face became even more set. He dropped his head and seemed to slump in the chair.

I looked back at my dishes. "Jon," Jerry said, "understand this. We're just going to talk about it once. The accident was just one of those things that happen sometimes when people are working together. You were my helper and you're a good worker. It just happened. So don't blame yourself. Let's forget it. I'm going to be fine, and we'll cut more limbs together, okay?"

Out of the corner of my eye I saw Jon sit up straighter. He got up and walked around to his daddy and just leaned against him. No one spoke—not even me—but I knew this was Jon's way of saying, "Thanks, Dad. I'm sorry." Jerry put his left arm around Jon. After a few minutes, they parted. Jon went outside. Jerry left the table and I cleared away the dishes, wondering if Jerry's few, simple words of forgiveness had made an impression on Jon. Had Jerry let him off too lightly?

The weeks passed rapidly. We didn't discuss the accident anymore. About six weeks after it had happened, I had to get after Jon for continually being late for supper. I used a method of punishment that works well for our boys. I assigned him an essay to write. "You choose the topic," I added sternly. I knew what to expect. A theme entitled "Football" or "Airplanes."

Jon seemed unusually involved in the essay. He didn't even complain about my assigning it. He said very little. He just sat down at my desk, his head almost touching the paper, and began writing in his left-handed scrawl. After a while he handed me the essay and left the room. It read:

Forgiveness

When you forgive somebody, you mean that what they did is all right. When you do something wrong, you should ask God to forgive you. But He won't forgive you unless you ask Him in your heart. The Bible says you should forgive someone who has done wrong 490 times. That's seven times seventy. When they nailed Jesus to the cross and spit on Him and called Him names, He said, "Forgive them, Father, for they know not what they do." Now if Jesus can do that, then surely you can forgive somebody when they do something to bother you.

Forgiveness is a sign of kindness and love. When you ask God to forgive you, you must forget completely about it. When you sin, you must always ask for forgiveness because if you don't you will be asked in heaven why you didn't. When you forgive somebody, do it because you love them, not just to be good.

So the next time you forgive somebody, remember why you're doing it. And always forgive others.

I gave Jon his first A on an essay even though it had misspelled words.

"Thanks, Mom," he beamed when he saw the grade. I nodded, wishing there were a higher mark than an A.

That night at supper I somehow spilled Jon's glass of milk all over the table, his plate, and him. I sat there for a moment in silent disbelief, thinking, Mothers don't spill milk. Jon smiled with the milk dripping down his shirt and said quietly, "That's okay, Mama. I have to take a bath anyway, and you know I don't like milk. It wasn't really your fault." Then he jumped up and grabbed a towel.

Everyone at the table lowered their eyes, but I saw them smiling. I smiled, too, and felt happy on the inside even though the milk was dripping all over the just-waxed kitchen floor. Forgiveness must work more miracles, large and small, than anything else in the world . . . or in the home.

A Lesson in Childlike Faith

THERESE MARSZALEK

My children had never been to a baseball game before, so I was thrilled when my husband surprised us with tickets to a Mariners' game. Although I wasn't fond of sports in general, I was excited about this opportunity. We packed up our three children and set out for the Seattle Kingdome.

The kids chattered endlessly as we settled into our seats. My excitement was quickly tempered, however, when I overheard a conversation between some men seated behind us. Their loud discussion was peppered with curse words. I cupped my hands over my children's ears in a futile attempt to protect them from the foul language.

How can people talk like that, I wondered, *when they can see there are small children right in front of them?*

I couldn't resist the temptation to see who was saying those filthy words. Trying my best to be subtle, I twisted around to discover a row of several scruffy men guzzling beer. "Oh boy, I can see we're in for a real treat today," I grumbled, turning around stiffly in my seat.

After we stood and sang the national anthem, we were treated to an astounding fireworks display. The kids were mesmerized by the flare of color and light. The crowd applauded loudly when the announcer said that the fireworks would be displayed every time the Mariners hit a home run. Our own family cheering section shouted gleefully. Hoping to witness a continuous blast of fireworks, our expectant children wanted endless home runs.

We settled back into our seats to watch the game. Joe, only one year old at the time, had a difficult time sitting still and stared curiously at the characters behind us. He appeared to be amused by the loud men, and he continuously shot bright smiles at them through the bottle of juice hanging from his mouth.

Although I attempted to ignore the distractions behind us, I could not avoid hearing the shouts and obscenities that intensified as the game continued. Our irritating neighbors were obviously disgusted with the performance of our team, and they made it known to anyone within earshot. I desperately wanted to silence these ignorant men, but I couldn't think of what to say. I silently asked God to give me the proper words. As I fumed, I was keenly aware that the hostile words in my mouth were not from God, so I begrudgingly chose to stay quiet.

Inning after inning passed with no score. The men behind us displayed mounting irritation with the Mariners' lack of success. As one stood up to shout and shake his fist at the team, his beer toppled over, spilling it on himself and the floor beneath him. I looked down in disbelief, watching as the beer trickled down to our level. My purse was quickly saturated underneath my seat. *Great,* I thought. *What next?*

My husband and our oldest son were having some special father/son time together. No other family members appeared to be as concerned with our neighbors' behavior as I was. I realized this was a trial I would have to work through on my own.

Our three-year-old daughter, Emily, was still dwelling on the fireworks display we had seen earlier. She desperately wanted to see the fireworks again and was growing impatient and disgruntled. Her patience depleted, she could not resist the temptation to start whining. "I want to see the fireworks, Mommy," she complained, stomping her feet. "I want to see them right now."

I explained to Emily that the fireworks would not be displayed until our team hit a home run. This explanation soothed her for only a moment before she started whining again.

Sitting in my beer-soaked environment, frustrated at my less-than-desirable surroundings, I found myself feeling anything but Christian. My patience had worn thin, and I couldn't bear to hear one more complaint from my strong-willed daughter or our drunken neighbors.

Gritting my teeth, I resisted the temptation to lose my temper. I bent down, whispering firmly in my daughter's ear, "OK, Emily, I know you want to see some fireworks, but they're not going to go off again until our team gets a home run. Why don't we pray and ask God to give our team a home run, and then you can see the fireworks, OK?"

Although this comment to Emily was halfhearted on my part, I felt I had successfully put her off a bit longer. It was the ninth inning, and I was thankful this experience was almost over. My suggestion did not put Emily off, but instead brought a bright smile to her face. Emily welcomed the idea of asking God for help.

We joined hands and closed our eyes, and Emily said, "Dear God, I want to see the fireworks, and I can't see them unless our team gets a home run. Please make our team get a home run so that I can see the fireworks. Thank you, God. In Jesus's name, Amen." Emily sat back in her seat, satisfied with her prayer and appearing to have no further concern about the fireworks.

The next batter from our team stepped up to the plate. There were two men already on base. He swung the bat on the first pitch and slammed a home run right over the wall!

Music blared during the blazing fireworks display as

the fans cheered wildly. My mouth hung open as I watched the batter run the bases. We scored three runs. Emily jumped up and down excitedly as she watched her coveted fireworks. She wasn't the slightest bit surprised that the batter had made that home run. She only enjoyed receiving the answer that God had given her. She'd had a request, made it known to God, and then, sitting back with no further anxiety, had trusted that God would take care of her need. She had prayed in faith and believed that God would move on her behalf. I, on the other hand, simply sat in amazement at her precious miracle.

On a day in which I expected to do no more than attend a baseball game, God gave me a valuable lesson in faith. A child trusts God without cluttering up his or her mind with reasoning, analyzing, and doubting, and we adults should strive to do the same. God showed Himself to Emily, a little child whose heart was loyal to Him. In an environment I didn't think God could be part of, He was undoubtedly there.

A Walk on the Beach

ROBIN ATHON
AS TOLD TO NANCY B. GIBBS

It had been a long week. Robin felt the need to get away from it all. She immediately thought about the beach house her father owned. She loved that place. It was located on Tybee Island, the ideal place where she thought she could find peace and serenity.

Early one morning, Robin decided to go for a walk on the beach. She had grown up in church, but as an adult she had pulled away from God. She wasn't serving Him as she knew she should. As she walked out the door, she grabbed her Walkman, turned the music up, and started walking.

After a while, Robin stopped to rest. She needed some time to enjoy the scenery and to take pleasure in the wonders of the ocean and the world around her. While walking, Robin couldn't hear the music clearly. She sat down for a few minutes.

Eventually Robin pulled the headphones from her ears. She decided she wanted to simply be quiet for a few minutes. She wasn't particularly listening for God's quiet voice when she sat down, but she wasn't surprised when God gave her an assignment.

Robin glanced down the beach and saw a woman sitting alone on a log. Robin felt a strange urging from the Holy Spirit. *Go tell that woman that Jesus loves her.* For a few seconds Robin tried to shake it off.

There's no way to do that, she thought.

But the Holy Spirit wouldn't leave her alone. *Go tell that woman that Jesus loves her.*

Against her better judgment, Robin stood up. She became anxious while trying to gain her composure. Robin hadn't been in tune with God in recent days, but there was no doubt in her mind that God had a job for her at that very moment. And that job was to tell a stranger on the beach that Jesus loves her. Robin had to make a quick decision. Would she shy away or be obedient to God's instructions?

Robin stammered her way toward the woman, fearing this stranger would think she was crazy and take off running if she approached her talking about God. But since Robin was convinced that God had a mission for her, she proceeded toward the woman.

"Hi," Robin said. "Where are you from?"

The lady answered her and Robin began to make more small talk. Then in a flash the small talk transitioned into a more serious matter.

"I was sitting over there and felt I was supposed to come tell you something," Robin announced.

The lady looked up at Robin strangely. "What are you supposed to tell me?" the lady asked.

"I am supposed to tell you that Jesus loves you," Robin uttered. "I don't know why."

The lady began to cry. Robin cried along with her when the lady explained why God sent that message to her.

"My son died three years ago today," the woman explained. For a few minutes two strangers shared a miracle that neither will ever forget.

As she walked away, Robin felt a burst of excitement for spiritual things. She realized that God had used her to take a message to someone with a need. Robin ran back to the beach house as quickly as she could. She had to call her mother to share the miracle with her. God was more real to Robin at that moment than He had been in a long time.

Amazing Love

GREG ASIMAKOUPOULOS

Life is pretty typical for Eve Losh these days. With a ten-month-old in tow she struggles to find enough hours in the day to get everything done. Her son Gabriel is an angel most of the time, but he does need to be fed, changed, and monitored as he crawls through their suburban Seattle home.

What makes life a bit atypical is that Eve is a single parent. As Eve rocks her son to sleep each night and sings him a lullaby, she rehearses in her head how she will one day tell him about his dad and their relationship. It is an amazing love story of which he is a continuing chapter.

Eve and Jonathan's story had a rather unlikely beginning. She was a high school senior in Seattle and he a third-year student at the University of Washington. When Eve's brother Nate discovered his sister needed a date to her senior prom, he made it known to his college friends, including his roommate, Jonathan. Because Jonathan had seen Nate's attractive sister while visiting their home on weekends, he was only too willing to agree. But it wasn't that easy. A couple of Nate's buddies wanted to be considered for the envied opportunity. Only after a game of rock, paper, scissors was Eve's date determined. Jonathan grinned like a cat who'd feasted on a canary.

"My dad reminds me how Jonathan's mouth dropped open as he stood in the entry way of our home and watched me descend the stairs in my prom dress," Eve recalls with a smile. "But as much as he was dazzled by what he saw, I was even more drawn to him. I still can picture in my head how handsome he was."

Thus began a courtship that would last four years. It was a romance that could best be described by the words "amazing love," for a number of different reasons. Within a few weeks of the prom, Jonathan left on a seven-week mission trip with Campus Crusade to Slovenia. Although it was difficult for Eve to be separated from someone she loved, it was a trip that conveyed to her how much Jonathan wanted to make his life count for Jesus.

In a letter he wrote while traveling with the ministry team, Jonathan described his experience abroad. He made reference to a young Slovenian he'd met named Vlado who lived for booze, women, and parties. "Through our times hanging out, he (Vlado) found out about my desire to save sex for marriage. This decision of mine troubled him deeply, for every time we would see each other, he seemed to have more questions about why, and how I had made that decision. Vlado truly wanted to listen to my testimony and beliefs on the subject of God's gift of marriage. Through our conversation I was able to share the gospel with him, telling him every day I get up and thank the Lord that I can be alive and for His salvation. He looked at me with eyes I will never forget and said, "I wish we'd met so much sooner, because I just don't have that joy."

Jonathan's passion to please the Lord was one of the primary qualities that attracted Eve to him. As they continued to date over the next couple years, Bible study, worship, and outreach continued to mark their growing relationship. According to Jonathan's mom, a spiritual sensitivity had been a part of his life since he was a boy.

"From the time he was eight years old he was interested in learning and talking about spiritual matters," Kandi Losh recalls. "His eighth grade Sunday school teacher at Newport Covenant Church helped him understand the importance of taking a stand for Jesus. From that time on he wasn't afraid to challenge his friends when he felt they were headed in the wrong direction. But that didn't translate into a self-righteous attitude toward others."

As a result, it wasn't a shock to those who knew him when Jonathan announced that he'd been hired for the interim youth director position at Newport Covenant. Even though he'd graduated from the University of Washington in 2000 with a degree in political science, he had a heart for serving Jesus and loving kids. While Eve plugged away at getting her degree, Jonathan plied his hand at youth ministry.

"Jonathan really jumped at the chance to serve his home church," Pastor Howard Burgoyne remembers. "He was particularly passionate about using his musical gifts to lead youth in worship. With Eve at his side, Jonathan had a burden to draw kids to the Lord. He also had a willingness to invest himself in what mattered most."

About the time Jonathan began working at Newport, he complained to his dad about intense headaches and occasional dizziness. David Losh, a physician, insisted that he be checked out. A series of tests were conducted over a few months. In August 2001, the doctors' diagnosis left Jonathan little room for doubt. He had an incurable brain tumor. Jonathan and his family were devastated.

The news blindsided the couple who were beginning to make plans for the future. Eve was about to begin her senior year at the University of Washington. After three years of dating, they'd begun to talk about marriage. Careerwise, Jonathan had dreams of becoming a poli-sci teacher in a local high school, while Eve fancied herself as a dental hygienist until kids came. She relished the thought of being a stay-at-home mom.

"I didn't view the doctors' verdict as a death sentence," Eve admits. "I was shocked but not hopeless. I knew people who had gotten brain cancer and recovered. My grandmother is one of them. In my heart I believed that through the doctors and prayer, Jonathan would be healed."

Jonathan privately wondered if his hopes to marry the love of his life would ever be realized. After all, who would be willing to marry someone who is terminally ill? However, three months after receiving his diagnosis, after much prayer and reflection (and six weeks of intense radiation treatments) Jonathan took the bold step of asking Eve to marry him.

"Of course, I said yes," Eve is quick to answer. "I never wavered in my desire to become Mrs. Jonathan Losh. The thought of standing by him and supporting him emotionally, physically, and financially actually energized me."

When Jonathan asked Eve's father if he had concerns about giving her hand to someone with an incurable brain tumor, her dad responded, "I have only two questions for you: do you love my daughter, and will you help her grow in her walk with the Lord?" The couple set a date to be married once Eve had graduated the following June.

"I'll call it amazing love," Howard observed. "Jonathan and Eve went through premarital counseling amid the continuous radiation treatments. I was blown away by their common poise and determination to proceed. All the time, they trusted God. At first I thought it might be denial, but I soon recognized it as faith in the sovereignty of God and an uncommon commitment to each other."

By mid-May of 2002, the impact of the cancer and six weeks of radiation treatments forced Jonathan to step down from his paid position. Although he continued to volunteer with the youth ministry whenever his energy allowed, his ability to concentrate and fully express his thoughts became increasingly difficult.

A month later, tests revealed accelerated growth in the malignant tissue. Because doctors also were troubled by a dangerous brain cyst, surgery was required right away. The outlook was grim.

"When I heard that Jonathan might only have two months to live, my confidence that he was going to beat this thing began to collapse," Eve candidly admits. "I couldn't help but wonder about God's purposes in it all. One of my roommates challenged me that my decision to marry Jonathan was not about living happily ever after but allowing myself to be the means through which God would provide for his needs."

Fearing that his days were numbered, Jonathan determined to know the joy of being married to this one he'd pursued for four years. He prevailed upon Eve to move their wedding up before the surgery. Instead of a full-blown service in the church, they opted for a ceremony on June 10 with family in the Losh's backyard bordered by azaleas and rhododendrons.

"Saying our vows was a powerful experience," Eve confessed. "It's easy for most people to gloss over the 'in sickness and in health, till death do us part' section. We took those words seriously because we knew we were in the midst of the worst kind of sickness and probably facing death in the near future."

Three days later, doctors wheeled Jonathan into surgery while the family huddled in the waiting room asking the Lord to spare his life. Within several hours the word came back that the surgical team had accomplished what they'd hoped. There were still parts of the tumor that could not be removed, but it appeared that prayers for an extension to Jonathan's life would be answered.

For the week-long recovery, Eve never left her patient-husband's side. The nursing staff was amazed at the love they witnessed between the newlyweds. They even taped a makeshift sign to the door that said HONEYMOON SUITE.

Twelve days after this most recent surgery, Jonathan marshalled his strength and donned a tuxedo. Standing beside his gown-clad bride, they celebrated their commitment to marriage in a ceremony at Newport Covenant Church.

The honeymoon in Hawaii for which they had planned would actually have to wait for a year. It was a hard year of treatments and emotional ups and downs. Still, for those who watched Jonathan's determination to fight the enemy cells within his body, it was a year of triumph.

"It was a triumph because of how he taught those around him how to live life to the fullest," Jonathan's father, Dave, insists. "He never complained. He did not dwell on why this was happening to him and did not become angry or morose. Whenever I would see him, there would be a smile and a friendly word even in the most discouraging of times."

The ten days Jonathan and Eve spent in Hawaii during the summer of 2003 was everything he'd imagined. Bright, sunny days. Warm, tropical nights. Good eating and the chance to fulfill a longtime dream.

For the next eighteen months, life for Jonathan became increasingly a challenge. The chemo ceased to arrest the tumor's growth and Jonathan lost the ability to speak. Still, Eve and Jonathan remained resolute in their determination to battle the cancer as a team. Resisting the temptation to hole up and withdraw, they welcomed the opportunity to plug in to a Bible study group from church.

"In hindsight I can see how the Lord overcame our reluctance to join a group, with Jonathan as sick as he was," Eve admits. "At first, connecting with people we didn't know all that well was quite uncomfortable. But those virtual strangers quickly became cherished friends. They provided us with an amazing support system of prayer and encouragement that we both leaned on for survival."

On Thanksgiving Day 2004 the family gathered around Jonathan's bed. They were grateful he had beat the odds and lived as long as he had. They were also extremely thankful that Jonathan had been blessed with a

godly wife whose amazing love was defined by her tire-
less devotion and continual optimism. Although Jonathan
was unable to say anything, he attempted to be a part of
the family activities. In spite of intense headaches
throughout the day, he smiled at Eve. The next day
Jonathan slipped into a semi-comatose state that would
last nearly a month.

On December 19, a week before the tsunami in South
Asia resulted in the deaths of nearly a quarter-million people,
Jonathan died quietly in the presence of those who had kept
watch over his last days.

But that is not the end to this amazing love story. The
story of faith and hope Eve will one day tell her son has a
remarkable postscript. When it became obvious to
Jonathan that God's answer to his prayers for healing
would be answered by a whole body in heaven, he
expressed his desire to his wife that she be left with a tan-
gible reminder of their love for each other. He wanted to
provide for the means that Eve could one day have a child
by him. They told no one.

On Valentine's Day 2005, eight weeks after Jonathan's
death, Eve announced to her parents and in-laws that she
was pregnant through artificial insemination. Eight months
later on September 20, 2005, Eve gave birth to a healthy
baby boy. She named him Gabriel Jonathan Losh.

"Words cannot describe the joy our grandson is to us,"
Kandi admits with a smile. "He truly is Jonathan's little

angel and God's gracious gift to our family. Gabriel is a living reminder of a son we will never forget and living proof of Jonathan and Eve's amazing love."

CHAPTER 2

Before You Even Ask

And now I have everything, and more. I have all I need. . . . My God will use his wonderful riches in Christ Jesus to give you everything you need (Philippians 4:18–19 NCV).

Wouldn't it be great if you could see into your future and know what you would need to ask God for in advance? Well, not to worry! God *can* see into your future, and He knows what you will need in advance. That's why He often sends answers to your prayers . . . before you even ask.

Always on Time

RHONDA BROWN

Diego was the first-born grandchild of David and Rhonda Brown. The three-year-old was a beautiful specimen of the blending of his two ethnic heritages, his father Hispanic, his mother Caucasian. Rhonda and David adored him and kept him often out on their farm located in the middle of nowhere, miles from the nearest town.

Diego loved to wander the farm, talking to the animals in his precious Spanish-English child-speak. However, David and Rhonda watched him like a hawk, and he was never allowed to cross the fences into the cow pasture or the horse corral.

One day, as the grandparents lounged on their big front porch enjoying the antics of Diego, they both leapt to their feet at the same time and screamed, "Diego, no!" The toddler had wandered near the horse corral and was bending over picking up something from the grass.

Just as Diego stood, a horse ran near the fence, thrust its hooves through the barbed wire and gave two strong kicks: one to Diego's face, and one to his head. He lay bleeding and unconscious by the time his grandparents reached his side.

"Let's roll him in a blanket and get him to town," David ordered. "We can get there before an ambulance can get here." They did so and Rhonda held the still child in her arms as David sped down the long driveway to the county road. Holding the office of County Commissioner, David was on his radio ordering roads to be cleared and escorts on hand for their race to the hospital.

Before they reached the end of their driveway, an ambulance careened into the lane. Three EMTs jumped out to assess the situation. They bundled Diego into the ambulance and helped Rhonda climb aboard.

"How did you know?" stuttered David. "We didn't call 911."

"We don't have a clue, sir," replied the EMT. "We were headed back to town from a country run and something, or someone, told our driver to head for your house, which she did, and your situation is what we found. Thank God, I'd say."

"Thank God, indeed," mumbled David as he jumped in his truck to follow the ambulance to town.

They arrived in time to apply life-saving techniques to Diego's battered face and head. The doctors later attested, as they proudly oversaw the grandson's discharge from the hospital, that had the ambulance not been immediately available, Diego would not have survived.

Today, at nearly four, Diego bears no scars, no brain damage, and best of all, no fear of horses! God is always on time.

Be Still

ELIZABETH SCHMEIDLER

My vacuum nearly flew across the living room rug in my hope to cross another chore off my mental "to do" list. Like most other days, I had much to get accomplished in a short amount of time, but strangely, I was somewhat enjoying the time with only my thoughts and the rhythmic humming of the vacuum. So relaxed was I, that I was quite taken by surprise when the words, "Be still" rose up inside of me. *How strange,* I thought, and dismissed the phrase immediately.

They came again, this time more firmly. "BE STILL." I paused my forward vacuum stroke and waited a few seconds before I chuckled and audibly mumbled, "I'm not nervous Lord; I'm just vacuuming." I quickly resumed vacuuming.

"BE STILL."

Third time. Now, I'm really listening, and my heartbeat is increasing just a bit, so I flipped off the vacuum switch and stood still in the living room.

"What is it, Lord?" I asked, now knowing for sure that I needed to listen to this inner prompting.

"BE STILL."

Quickly my mind raced to pinpoint where my husband and children were and whether they could be in trouble. But somehow, I just knew that they were okay. This puzzled me further. The inner awareness of God's voice had come to me many times before when my kids were sick in the night, when I wrote poetry, or a friend needed me, but it usually happened amid a quiet time and usually during my prayers. Never had I experienced His prompting in the midst of noise, such as now. I knew something was up.

For several moments, I just stood there in the middle of my living room, the vacuum still in one hand, my heart beating ever faster. Suddenly, a lightbulb moment occurred, and I set the vacuum upright. Thoughts were forming quickly in my mind as I rushed down the hallway to my desk in our spare bedroom. There, in plain sight, was a copy of my poem, "Be Still," which I had written over two years before. It was lying there because I had been experimenting with different print styles while making a copy for the local Christian bookstore, which had recently ordered a copy for one of their customers. With trembling hands I picked up the poem and headed back to my piano in the living room.

For two weeks I had been working on, and had completed, a melody that had popped into my head. This melody was both a delight and a surprise since it had only been several months prior that I discovered, much to my complete astonishment, that I could write piano music and songs. This, in itself, was a miracle to me because I don't have any formal music training other than five months of piano lessons in the fifth grade. One day, however, my two hands began playing together and my first song, "Come Fill Me," was born. Since that first song, I had written only one other song that started with words first and then the melody.

For some reason, however, I had been unable to come up with words to this latest melody on which I had been so steadfastly working, and though friends and family had made several good suggestions, I was determined to wait until God revealed the lyrics to me. In fact, I was so convinced to wait until I felt sure of what God wanted from my melody, that I had completely forgotten about it.

As my hands began to softly play my new composition, I whispered, "No way." Then, louder, "You've got to been kidding me . . ." Though my mind could not comprehend what was happening, my heart knew that the words to my "Be Still" poem were going to fit perfectly into the music I had written. Sure enough, perfectly. I didn't have to change a word, a phrase, a note. Tears trickled down my cheeks while I began to sing the words, because I knew that I had just witnessed a miracle. One just can't fit already created words into a melody without first "tweaking" it. Most song lyrics are written with a melody in mind, or else the melody is created around the words. In other words, you can't shove the words to "The Star-Spangled Banner" into the melody of "Twinkle, Twinkle, Little Star" or "Amazing Grace."

My tears ran freely now as my mind slipped back to the time when I had written the poem. I had just gone through several months of not knowing what was wrong with my stomach and digestive system, and I had undergone surgery and had seen several different doctors before getting things straightened out. One day, with my curling iron in one hand and mascara wand in the other, I felt the prompting to quit what I was doing and sit down at the computer to write. Sure enough, God helped me pour out all my thoughts about my prior illness experience into the poem, "Be Still." After the poem was completed, I read it aloud and thought to myself, "This would make a great song."

Never . . . in a million, trillion years would I have thought that it would be *me* to write the song! At this point in time, I didn't even know that I could play the piano, let alone write songs.

God just keeps changing me, and I am humbled every time, every day, every moment that I realize how many times He's made the impossible happen in my life. No matter what life throws my way, I know beyond all things, that He is real, ever-present, all-knowing, and that I am, indeed, blessed.

Be Still

I'm amazed beyond all measure, that You could think
  of me . . .
That You could know my thoughts and hurts, and
  what is meant to be.

I sometimes take for granted, all the wonders of the
  earth . . .
The beauty of the flowers and trees, the joy of living
  birth.

I can gaze upon Your splendor, while birds soar
  through the air . . .
Yet not believe Your promises, or know how much
  You care.

At times it's hard to see, and still harder yet to feel,
Your loving arms around me . . . to know You're at
  the wheel.

If only for a moment, I would reach my hands to
  You . . .
You'd guide my way, my steps, my life, in a way
  that's good and true.

You'll guide my thoughts and actions, if I will just be
    still.
You'll show my heart and mind and soul, what is to
    be Your will.

Help, oh Lord, my unbelief, my doubting heart and
    mind . . .
And let me rest within Your care, knowing peace is
    what I'll find.

A Meal for a Miracle

SUE FERGUSON

Placing the phone thoughtfully on the cradle, I felt uneasy. The call I'd just received was to announce the recent arrival of a new baby. "It's a boy!" was the enthusiastic squeal. A child is a gift from God, so of course that was good news, but my excitement was held in check by an overwhelming realization. Taking a meal to friends after the birth of a baby is a way I meet a need and share their celebration, but that day I was burdened with heaviness. My morning had already included a worried search through the nearly empty cupboards and refrigerator, wondering how I was going to feed my three young children and husband until payday. How could I prepare a meal appropriate to deliver as a gift and provide for the needs of my own family too?

Making a quick call to my husband, hard at work, I explained the dilemma. With no hesitation, he quietly instructed me, "Go ahead and prepare their dinner. I'll deliver it tonight." Once again I hung up the phone with uneasiness. This time, though, I felt the comfort of joint determination. I wanted to give a meal. My husband also desired for us to provide for our friends. I would follow his guidance. After all, we could eat rice or cereal; I knew we weren't going to starve.

With resolve, I swallowed hard as I planned, shopped, and prepared a meal that afternoon, my three children at my side. Later, my husband took dinner to our friends. Whatever we ate after his delivery that night wasn't memorable, but the next afternoon was one we'll never forget!

My husband and I prayerfully planned to make do with the few remaining ingredients in the cupboard. The plain and basic meals would satisfy us until a trip to the grocery store was affordable. God had provided for us in the past; we would trust Him now.

Afternoon came. The phone rang.

"Hello."

My frazzled neighbor and casual friend began, "Sue, the movers are coming soon. Would you be willing to take the remaining food from my freezer?"

"Sure, do you want me to run over and get it now?"

"No, we'll drive over in a few minutes; that'll be easier for everyone. Thanks so much!"

She thanked me? Already I was visualizing what my freezer would look like if our family had been preparing to move . . . perhaps a half-empty bag or two of veggies, a boxed pizza, and a pound of ground beef. Maybe a can of frozen orange juice too. Sounded good to me!

The door bell rang and I went to greet my neighbors.

All four family members stood at my door holding grocery bags overflowing with ice-cold food. Rushed
because the moving van was in their driveway, they
quickly came in and deposited the paper bags on my
kitchen table. As the dad went to the car to bring in one
final bag, we shared hugs and said our good-byes.

Closing the door, I went to the table to unpack my
groceries and organize them for my freezer and that
night's dinner. Each time I reached into a bag I was more
amazed. Soon, with my hands shaking and my voice
breaking with emotion and delight, I called my husband.

"It's obvious the Clarksons didn't include eliminat-
ing food in the freezer as part of their moving plan. They
just brought over five bags of food! I can't believe it;
there is so much food—great food we never buy—steak,
shrimp, fruit, and ice cream treats!"

I didn't have to say more. The Clarksons may not
have had a plan for the food in their freezer, but we both
knew God had. Since that day, we've never questioned
the appropriateness of sharing a meal or doubted God's
willingness to provide for us with a miracle.

Lost in the Fire

MARY HOLLINGSWORTH

A bilene Christian University is my alma mater—a relatively small Christian college in West Texas with a strong academic program and a friendly atmosphere. I enjoyed my four years as an undergraduate and received my degree in the spring of 1970. In fact, I liked ACU so much that I stayed an extra year, worked for the university in public relations, and began my master's degree program. However, after five years I decided it was time for me to venture out into the real world, so I moved to Arlington, Texas, and went to work for Hunt Oil Company in Dallas.

While I was at ACU my parents lived in northern Arkansas, where my dad was a minister. Soon after I moved to Arlington, Dad was invited to move to Mansfield, Texas—about fifteen minutes from my apartment in Arlington—and work with a church there. So, for the first time in several years, we were living close together again. And I looked forward to dropping in for Mom's great cooking from time to time.

In a couple of weeks Mayflower Moving Company arrived to move my parents. The front half of the truck was already loaded with another family's belongings, so they put my folks' furnishings in the back half of the truck. Then they left Fayetteville and started the long haul down through the mountains and across Texas to Mansfield.

Meanwhile, Mom and Dad drove their two cars from Arkansas to Texas, filled with some of their most breakable and personal items. Since the moving company had said it would be two or three days before they actually arrived in Mansfield, Mom and Dad stopped in East Texas to see my granddad. And the next day they drove on through the Dallas–Fort Worth metroplex to Mansfield, where they unloaded the two cars at the new house.

I had gone to work that day, but I was looking forward to having dinner with them that evening. So I hurried home after work and changed clothes, eager for them to come. My apartment mate, Nancy, was already home when I arrived and had turned on the television to watch the news. So I sat down to watch with her while I waited for my folks.

Suddenly, in the middle of the newscast, the commentator began telling the story of a moving van that had turned over in the median of the Dallas–Fort Worth Turnpike and caught fire. On the screen appeared disastrous video coverage of the huge van on its side and in flames. And having moved as many times as we had, I thought, *Those poor people.*

Then the commentator said, "Household goods on

the Mayflower van belonged to two families—George and Helen Mathews of Gateway, Arkansas, and Clyde and Thelma Shrode of Fayetteville, Arkansas."

Clyde and Thelma Shrode. Clyde and Thelma Shrode. No! It couldn't be!

"That's my folks, Nancy! That's their moving van!"

We sat frozen to our seats, listening to the rest of the distressing report. The van had developed engine trouble, and the engine had caught fire. When that happened, the driver lost control of the giant rig and went off the freeway into the large ditch between the east and west roadways. Then the van flipped onto its side, and fire spread to the trailer and its contents.

The commentator noted that a few of the belongings on the truck had been saved, but most of the goods were a total loss. Fortunately, the driver was not injured. But the traffic on the turnpike was backed up for almost seventeen miles while the fire fighters worked to extinguish the fire, remove the burned-out truck, and haul away what was left of two families' lives.

"Oh, Mary, that's just awful!" said Nancy. "What can we do? Where are your folks?"

"I don't know. They're supposed to be here any minute. I wonder if they even know what's happened."

I jumped up and ran to the phone, but I had no idea how to reach them (this was pre–cell phone days). I called the church in Mansfield, but no one answered since it was after office hours. Then I pulled out the phone book to look up the number of the moving company, but about that time there was a knock on the door.

Nancy got up and opened the door to find my parents had arrived.

"Mom, Dad," I said, coming to hug them, "we just saw a news report . . . "

"Yes, we know all about it, honey," said Dad. "It's a disaster . . . but we'll get through it. Don't worry. The most important thing is that the driver didn't get hurt."

Over dinner, my parents related other details about the accident they had been given by the police and the moving company. The best news was that, because my parents' belongings had been at the back of the van, some of their things had been saved. But, at that point, they didn't know what those items were.

My dad was especially concerned because his sermon outlines for more than thirty years and his entire preaching library were on the truck—a disastrous situation for a minister starting a new job. And his library contained many turn-of-the-twentieth-century books given to him by an old preaching mentor of his. Those books were priceless and irreplaceable.

Mom was sad about losing family treasures like photos, handmade quilts her mother had made before she died, antique picture frames, antique furniture my dad had refinished, and other special keepsakes.

Mom said, "And we had a whole houseful of new furniture—three bedroom suites, living room furniture, and new appliances. It was the first new furniture we'd had in more than thirty years." It was so new, in fact, that I had never even seen it.

"Fortunately, though," Dad said with a weak smile, "we had full insurance coverage, so we should come out all right . . . except for my sermons and books and the family keepsakes, of course. No amount of money can replace those."

The next day Mom and Dad went to the moving company's warehouse where their rescued furnishings had been taken after the fire. There they faced a dismal pile of burned and scorched items. But that's also where they experienced the miraculous love of God.

There in the middle of the burned mess sat my dad's desk, in perfect condition. And in the middle desk drawer were all his sermon outlines untouched. God surely knew he would need those in order to carry on His work.

Nearby was Dad's complete library, and even though the books smelled like smoke and one of the bookcases was broken, they were not otherwise damaged. God knew he needed those, too, no doubt.

Mom found several boxes of family pictures, her mother's quilts, and other treasures. What a relief!

When everything had been inventoried, we were astonished to find that all the new furniture and appliances had been burned up. But since they were new, Mom and Dad had no sentimental attachment to them anyway. The insurance money would completely replace them. But most of the irreplaceable and special treasures had been saved, which to us was evidence of God's loving care and protection. After all, fire is not selective in what it burns. The only way that fire could have burned the new and left the old is if it were being directed by a divine baton, like a flaming symphony.

It took weeks and months for my parents to work through the insurance claims, have broken antiques repaired, and air out the smoky smell from dad's books and the other things they managed to save. It was a huge mess, but my parents struggled through it with godly patience and good humor.

Through the years, when Mom or Dad would look for some familiar kitchen item or tool but couldn't find it, they would simply say, "I guess that got lost in the fire." And through that experience and their gracious acceptance of it, I learned to see material things as temporary and mostly replaceable, an understanding that has served me well in our temporary world.

We Believe in Miracles...
and CPR

BARBARA CURTIS

L ast summer I almost lost a son. I was finishing up errands when I got the call on my cell phone. Thank God for cell phones! The voice was calm, insistent, pressing the words into focus. My five-year-old son, Jesse, in trouble. A near-drowning. Helicopter on its way. No time for me to get there. Call back in five minutes to find out which hospital.

I hung up, not quite breathing, and dialed my husband, Tripp's, cell phone.

He said, "Barbara, what's happening? There's a helicopter over our house!" He was pulling into our driveway. Thank God one of us would be there!

Then I was alone with all the questions: *How had this happened? Had someone forgotten to lock the gate?*

Would he live? Jesse's sweet smile, almond eyes, and silky brown skin seemed suddenly more real, more necessary than the sidewalk under my feet. The EMT had said something about brain damage. Oh, no, if Jesse—

already challenged with Down's syndrome—should have to work harder than he already does!

Tripp had a better perspective: "Thank God, he's alive," he said when he called back. Thank God for close calls, moments of reprieve, and maybe a miracle.

Jesse was already whirring above the San Francisco Bay to Children's Hospital in Oakland. Thank God, he'd be there before I could even get on the freeway.

With no traffic, it would take me an hour. It was time to reassure my kids via cell phone and to hear the whole story.

Jesse hadn't been alone. Everyone was swimming, but no one heard when he'd somehow slipped off the seat in the hot tub where little kids like to hang out. He went under without a sound.

My oldest son, Josh, spotted him and pulled him out like a soggy rag doll. Jesse's skin was blue, his eyes rolled back, his chest still.

"We need to do CPR!" Matt said.

And the two oldest brothers went to work—opening the airway, giving two quick breaths, checking for the pulse. Then, because there was no pulse, chest compressions. Ben called 911. Thank God, he called them first! Thank God, my children showed common sense. Thank God, Josh and Matt knew CPR!

And here's why those inclined to believe in Providence see life filled with more intentional meaning than those who think in terms of simple twists of fate:

In 1995 Tripp and I were required to pass a CPR course in order to adopt Jesse. For some strange reason, we decided to have our whole family trained. I say strange because, at the time, Josh and Matt were only twelve and eleven and we had no pool. Recreational water play consisted of blowing up an inflatable circle, filling it with a few inches of water, then spending hours looking for leaks. Not much chance of drowning there.

Now, five years later, Josh and Matt saved Jesse's life —this according to the EMTs who converged on our house, rounded up the kids, secured the dogs, called me, and arranged for Jesse's transport.

Still, I think there's a little something else involved.

Anne Lamott once said of miracles, "It's not just that I believe in them; I rely on them." I can relate—just as I relate to the words of Job in the Bible: "He performs wonders that cannot be fathomed, miracles that cannot be counted."

In Jesse's story I see a few myself. Jesse regained consciousness after twenty-seven hours, then developed a virulent pneumonia. The going was slow until his fourth day, Sunday, when after a particularly cranky, distressing morning, Jesse suddenly sat up, smiled, and wanted to play. A week later he was completely healed.

When we called our CPR instructor to let him know our training had already saved a life, he was amazed. Though he'd been training people for fifteen years, this was a first for him. What's more, even in his primary job as a firefighter he's arrived on thousands of accident scenes and never seen someone already doing CPR.

And though he himself has initiated CPR on twenty-six of those scenes, none of the victims survived.

That's because it was too late. The first five minutes after someone stops breathing are critical—too short a time to wait for the professionals. Since 75 percent of the time the person who needs CPR will be someone you know, knowing how to help means more safety for your family.

It did for ours.

Jesse—whose name means "God exists"—almost died, and didn't. But sometimes miracles aren't as simple as they look. Sometimes they depend on decisions we've made before.

Thank God we decided to have our family trained in CPR!

Comfort Zone

FAITH GRAY

W hen I was about ten years old my parents and I moved into a new house they had designed and built in Jackson, Mississippi. We loved our new home and were enjoying settling into our new environment.

About six months after moving in, my mom began to complain of pain in her joints. Initially, the pain was in her shoulders, but within a few months it had spread to all her joints, and she was no longer able to work. She was soon diagnosed with severe rheumatoid arthritis.

When I was eleven years old my mom spent a full month in the Baptist Hospital receiving treatments and medications for her pain. When she finally came home she was barely able to move without help. At least three times each week she had to go to the hospital for physical therapy. Since it was summertime and I was out of school, I was responsible for helping her out of bed, bracing her against the wall, and dressing her. It would then take us about fifteen minutes to get out of our house and into the taxi to go to the hospital. After her therapy, the process was reversed, and I would get her home and back into bed.

Mom's existence was spent in agonizing pain. I would hear her crying at night when she and Dad thought I was asleep. Sadly, Mom's doctor couldn't give her any encouragement about being cured or ever having a better quality of life. One of her friends told her she had heard that climate changes sometimes helped improve arthritis and regain mobility, but her doctor told her that wasn't really true and encouraged her just to learn to live with her limitations.

Not ready to give up, my parents started researching cities in more arid parts of the country. One day I found a newspaper from Albuquerque, New Mexico, in their bedroom, and I asked them about it. They told me we were going there on our vacation in a few weeks. When vacation time arrived, my dad and I drove to Albuquerque and settled into a motel. Mom stayed with friends until we were ready for her to come out. Then she took the plane trip alone to join us.

Mom had a lot of trouble changing planes at Dallas Love Field because she could hardly move and was in such pain. She was glad to finally land in Albuquerque and get into bed to rest. After two or three days of rest, she was feeling better, so my parents and I began driving around looking at houses. Dad also started looking for job opportunities and had some interviews. Three different companies told him they would love to have him come to work for them if we moved there.

On Sunday we found a church that seemed promising as a church home for us. My folks, being the friendly people they were, made friends instantly with some of the church members.

By the time we had been in Albuquerque a week, Mom was actually able to get out of bed on her own and walk around without much assistance. She was so excited to be able to walk instead of using a wheelchair and not have to depend so much on pain medications. By the time we had to return to Mississippi, Mom was about 80 percent improved and was so mobile it was hard to believe she had been so incapacitated before.

Within two weeks of being back in Mississippi, Mom was once again bedridden and in severe pain, and I was back to standing her against the wall to dress her. So, after much prayer and soul searching, my parents decided we would move to Albuquerque. They took a major step of faith and put our house up for sale. When the house was sold, my dad gave his two-week notice at the job he had held all of my life. We packed up our household goods and made arrangements to place everything in storage until we had a new house. By this time, I had started the seventh grade and was getting settled into junior high school life.

Just before we were to leave Jackson, one of my dad's brothers called and asked Dad if he was determined to move to Albuquerque. Dad told him we really needed to move to a drier climate and asked him why he was asking. Uncle Joe said he had just heard about a job opening in El Paso, Texas, and he thought Dad might like to check into it. Dad said he would consider detouring through El Paso because he wanted to pursue any options God had for him. Finally one morning we climbed into our car and left our hometown, family, and friends behind, heading to Albuquerque by way of El Paso.

The car trip was long and tedious, since Mom was with us this time. We had to make many stops so she could get out and move around. It took us about four days to make the trip. On the evening we drove into El Paso on Highway 80, it was raining cats and dogs. The streets were flooding, and we had trouble finding a motel.

Mom looked at Dad and told him to keep on driving. She said, "If this is dry, I don't want to see wet!"

Dad smiled and said we had to stop for the night anyway, so let's see what would happen. The next day the sun was shining, but it was still humid—just not as humid as Mississippi. We got settled into a motel with a kitchenette so I could cook our meals instead of eating out all the time.

Dad contacted the owner of the company Uncle Joe had told him about and set up a time for a job interview. He was offered the position immediately, but Dad said he had to discuss things with Mom first. After prayer and discussion, they decided to call about the potential jobs in Albuquerque. Each of the three companies Dad had talked with previously said they didn't currently have any openings, but they would try to find something for him if he moved there.

To Mom and Dad it seemed that God had closed the doors in New Mexico and opened a huge door in El Paso. So they took things one step further and looked for a rental house. We miraculously found one with no front steps, which was great for Mom but most unusual for a city built around a mountain.

We moved into our rented house in a couple of weeks. I got settled into the junior high school just three blocks from the house. And Dad's boss invited us to attend the Baptist church he and his family attended. Amazingly, we found a church home with only two steps up to the front doors. We were welcomed with open arms and settled into our new city and home.

By Christmas Mom was able to move freely and didn't require as much pain medicine. That spring my folks bought a house on the east side of the mountain. I was able to finish the school year at the same school, even though our new house was in a different school district. That summer we took a picture of my mom sitting cross-legged on the sidewalk of our home. She was now freely mobile and enjoying life to the fullest again.

The summer I turned thirteen, our life went back to normal. At church one night our pastor asked for personal testimonies. I broke the mold of being a very shy person and stood up to share our story with the congregation. I told them I believed God had used Mom's illness as a means to get us to move to El Paso, where He wanted us to live and serve Him.

Through the years my parents became surrogate parents to many young men and married couples stationed in El Paso at Fort Bliss and Biggs Air Force Base. I firmly believe that we were placed in El Paso for my folks to help all those young people who were far from home, lonely, and homesick. One of those couples was from East Tennessee, and I still have a close sisterly relationship with them thirty-nine years later.

Mom and Dad have gone to heaven now, but their legacy of love lives on in the lives of all those young people to whom they opened their hearts and home all those years ago. Those lives wouldn't have been the same if we had stayed in Jackson in our comfort zone.

Now when I go through hard times, I remember Mom's illness and the many blessings that came out of it. I know that God is in control, and I only need to trust Him. I pray that God will be able to use my life to bless others as He did my parents.'

Everyday Miracles

DONNA LOWICH

I believe in miracles, plain and simple. But are there plain and simple miracles? Yes, I believe that, too. For example, there was the time when our cat, Lucky (not quite five years old at the time) disappeared from our house on a cold, blustery January day. He managed to open the sliding glass door and stepped out to investigate the world around him.

His natural cat curiosity may have gotten the better of him, but he should have at least checked the weather forecast before venturing forth. He chose a wet, windy, and rather raw weekend to leave us. And leave us he did.

It wasn't just the weather we were worried about. Lucky wasn't used to being outside. (Even indoors, he preferred to be lying right next to the heat duct). Then there was the possibility of all sorts of animals in the woods to which he could fall prey. What would he eat? Lucky loved to eat but was partial to chicken, especially chicken cut up in tiny bits for him. Even though I was trying to keep everyone's mood as positive as possible, I knew the danger was very real.

We spent the entire weekend looking for him. Throughout the day on Saturday we busied ourselves by focusing on our only goal: find Lucky before the bad weather turned even worse. We each tried to put up a brave front for the others, but secretly we were all very worried and scared.

My son, Jeff, was fourteen at the time. Lucky was his cat, a gift from my husband, Walter, and me on his tenth birthday. Jeff was brokenhearted about the loss of the cat he had wished for since he was a small boy, the cat that had grown up with him.

I thought back to that first night in our house when Lucky was such a tiny bundle of fur with very blue eyes. I remembered the ride home after we chose Lucky (or was it the other way around?). He clung desperately to Jeff with his tiny claws piercing his T-shirt as Jeff tried to calm him down with whispered words and soothing strokes of kindly love. Upon our arrival home, the first instant his paws hit the floor, Lucky raced to the end table and surveyed the room from under its protective shelf.

To ease his fears, Jeff slept with him on the floor of his room for the first several nights. These memories urged me on to do what I could to find him.

So on and off throughout the day Walter and Jeff put on their boots and heavy jackets and walked through the woods in the back of our property, hoping that Lucky would magically appear despite the torrential rains and biting, heavy winds that brought havoc upon the area.

In the meantime, I worked the phone, calling area vets and shelters to see if Lucky had landed himself there. No such luck. No such Lucky.

On Sunday, our searching continued but still with the same discouraging results. By Sunday night we were planning our strategy for Monday. Walter and Jeff would go to the animal shelter in town before school. If he wasn't there, they'd file a report and a description, in case Lucky showed up later.

Hope faded as did daylight on Sunday. Tomorrow it was back to school and work, and we wouldn't be able to search with the intensity that we had during the weekend.

Monday morning brought more wind, more rain, but no Lucky. Walt went outside, calling Lucky's name, but was only answered by the howling wind.

Lucky was not at the shelter, so a report was filed. Walter took Jeff to school and returned home to make a flier describing Lucky. He delivered these fliers to every house on our street and the streets around us.

Monday passed with no word from either the shelters or the neighbors about Lucky. I phoned in a lost-and-found ad to the local newspaper. We all said some prayers that Lucky was all right. Jeff said it best: "Not knowing if he's okay is the worst part. If I just knew he was safe, in a house somewhere . . ." he left the rest of the sentence unfinished.

Tuesday passed; still no word about Lucky. Our worries increased as the weather for the following four days was forecast to be extremely cold, windy weather, with a snowstorm on Friday.

Wednesday came and there was still no sign of Lucky. The weather began its downward trend. By suppertime, the bone-chilling wind whistled through the bare branches of the trees at the rear of our yard, an ever-present reminder that our little cat was out there somewhere, lost, scared, and shivering from the cold.

Time for one last call to the shelter before it closes, I thought to myself.

"County Animal Shelter," said the bored voice on the other end of the phone. I recognized it as the same monotone voice of the man I had been speaking to every day since Friday.

"Uh, hi, again," I tried to maintain my composure. "I was just checking to see if anyone has brought in a white and gray tabby."

There was an audible sigh. "No, no one has brought in a gray and white tabby." It was again said in the same monotone with which I was greeted, but there was a sarcastic edge to it.

"I'm sorry to keep bothering you," I said by way of an apology, "but I'm desperate to find my son's cat."

Instead of dissuading him from continuing with his sarcasm, this seemed only to egg him on. "Well, why don't you say a prayer for your cat to return then?" he sneered.

I knew this wasn't meant as a comforting suggestion, but I wasn't about to let him know that.

"Thank you. I will."

I hung up the phone, and decided that this, indeed, was a great idea. Clearly, I wasn't making any headway on my own. I—we—needed some divine intervention.

I had a few moments of quiet solitude while preparing dinner in which to say my prayer. God would help, if I asked. I knew it. I felt it. Then I looked out the window into the gloomy darkness of a winter's night. I heaved a heavy sigh. The wind howled back its answer as I returned to making dinner.

During dinner we sat at the table and talked of what we would do tomorrow in case there was no response from either the neighborhood fliers or the newspaper ad. Then I thought I heard a faint cry outside. It was hard to tell because of the wind. Then I heard it again.

"Listen!" I said excitedly, straining to hear it again. "I think I hear Lucky! I think he's on the deck!"

Naturally, no one believed me. Walter and Jeff both scoffed at the idea, thinking it was my imagination working overtime. Then Walter said, "Wait. I think I hear it too."

That was it! That was all they needed. They both jumped into action. Jeff ran to the dining room doors that led to the deck. Walter ran down to the family room and got to the deck from the opposite direction. Sure enough, Lucky was huddled in a corner. But when he saw them, his fright increased, and he jumped off the deck and ran to hide under our neighbor's deck. Once they caught up with him, Lucky ran under the neighbor's car. Again, Walter and Jeffrey surrounded him. Lucky tried to run past Walter, who managed to grab him as he ran past.

He brought Lucky into the house. There was much excitement and celebrating going on downstairs. I was expecting to see an emaciated, dirty, wet, and trembling cat. As he strolled up the six stairs to the kitchen, I was amazed to see that he was perfectly dry and clean!

"It was," Walter said, "as if Lucky had just come back from a Club Med vacation." We marveled at how resourceful he was to protect himself from the wind-driven rain from the previous weekend.

The only sign that he had been away was that he was very hungry. Apparently, if he had caught anything to eat, no one showed up to cut it into small enough pieces for him to eat, so he did without instead. Coincidentally, for dinner that night we had roasted chicken, Lucky's favorite. He ate until he could eat no more.

Lucky followed Jeff's every move that night and for the next several nights. He made himself more sociable, as if to say, "Look, I'm here. If I'm not around, start looking for me!"

When they went upstairs to Jeff's room, I stopped and murmured a prayer of thanks for the return of our little cat, who truly needed a miracle. Actually, we all needed one.

Are We There Yet?

JOANNE K. HILL

When Sandy, my husband's sister, expressed a desire to stay in Indiana a little longer, he volunteered us to drive her back to New Jersey. Sandy's husband, Johnny, needed to go back to work, but they had only spent a few days with her family.

"I have some vacation time coming in a week." Ken figured. "Johnny can go back to work now. We'll drive out to your place next Friday."

Although Sandy was pregnant and we had three little ones, ages two, three, and four, I hastily agreed. Later, I had second thoughts.

"But Ken, where will we get the money?"

"Oh, we don't need much," he said. "You can pack some food, and we'll drive straight through. It will only take sixteen hours. Sandy can watch the kids while we take naps in the afternoon, so we can leave in the evening. That way the kids will sleep most of the trip. All it will cost is some gas, and Johnny gave me some money to help out."

Before long, I caught his infectious spirit of adventure. I always enjoyed seeing parts of this great country I had not seen before. Then, more worries popped into my mind.

"But what about our car? It's so old. We barely have room for the three kids in the back seat. Where will Sandy sit? And where will we put the luggage?"

Ken grinned. "Well, I plan to ask your dad if we can trade cars for those few days. His car is newer and I have a friend with a luggage rack we can strap on top. We can fit a kid in the front seat." Before I could protest, he added, "They can take turns. It will be fun."

I smiled but did not encourage Ken. Dad fastidiously cared for his automobiles. In addition, he was not a spontaneous guy like my husband. He planned trips carefully, sometimes for a whole year. Even day excursions required careful preparation with ample cash, emergency supplies, and a full tank of gas.

Surprisingly, Dad said yes. However, he gave one warning—again and again: "You must never let the gas gauge go past the halfway mark. If the needle lands on EMPTY, you are out of gas. There is *no* reserve."

Dad knew we would travel on some two-lane roads through mountains. As a state trooper, he helped many stranded motorists, which might be another reason he let us use his car rather than take off in our old one. Before letting us take the car, he had it completely serviced. Dad also bought a map, drawing a red marker along the best route, and asked us to call collect once we arrived. Repeatedly throughout his instructions, he cautioned both of us about letting the gas gauge go below the halfway mark.

The last words I heard as we pulled out of Dad's drive were, "Remember, you *must* get gas when the gauge is at the halfway mark. Otherwise, you will have no warning before you run out."

"Yes, sir!" Ken smiled and waved.

The next day, as Ken mowed the grass and prepared for leaving, I packed the car with all but the cooler and humans. Sandy watched the children while Ken and I caught some sleep. Right after a quick supper of cold-meat sandwiches and lemonade, we finished packing and hit the road.

A few minutes after we picked up our ticket at the Indiana tollbooth, the children cried in unison, "Are we there yet?"

"We won't be there until morning," Sandy said. "Why don't you see how many red cars you can find?"

The children enjoyed counting red cars, then blue cars, and finally big trucks. They colored in their books and drew pictures. We sang songs and made up stories. And we stopped at rest stops. Lots of them! At each stop, we checked the gas gauge. If the needle hovered anywhere near the halfway point, we filled the tank, while the three children and expecting mother emptied theirs.

After sunset the children grew sleepy and dozed off.

Shortly afterward, we came to a tollbooth. Three little heads popped up. "Are we there yet?" As we crossed from one state to the next, we always saw two tollbooths, one to pay and the next to receive a new ticket. Each time, at least one child's head popped up. "Are we there yet?"

Although we tried to coordinate the toll stops with service stations, the children never truly seemed to find their way to Dreamland. At the rest stop before the toll roads ended, I took the wheel.

"If driving gets too difficult, wake me up. I'll take over." Ken had taken a shorter nap than I had, and he looked it.

"Okay," I nodded as I checked the rearview mirror, but I felt confident that would not be necessary. The roads were wide enough and not too steep. Besides, I did not feel sleepy and I knew Ken needed the rest. As a mother, I had adjusted to taking catnaps, which I did along with the children between the many stops. Just before propping his head against a pillow on the window, Ken reminded me that the gauge registered nearly a quarter tank gone already.

"Watch for a service station." Even though Ken laughed at my dad's compulsiveness, he listened well.

I assured him I would.

Soon Ken snored in the passenger seat, but I still heard some grunts and moans from the children, as they jockeyed for position in the back. And our two-year-old sleeping in the front seat now, had roused a bit when we changed drivers.

Soon after I took over the driving, we encountered the two-lane mountainous roads Dad had pointed out on the maps. Fewer cars and less light greeted us. I wished for daylight so I could really see the beauty of the mountains, but gave thanks that all was quiet in the car. Yet I wondered if the children were sleeping soundly. Only a half hour had passed since we left the last toll stop.

I noticed a service station shortly after and glanced at the gas gauge. Although now past the quarter mark, the needle indicated some leeway before hitting the halfway marker. I decided to wait until the next station to fill up without disturbing anyone. The clock glowed 11:30 P.M.

An hour later, our car approached another service station. Closed! Another hour passed before I saw the next darkened station, apparently the last one on the highway, for after that only dark trees and an occasional car flashed by our windows.

Well, there has to be a service station up ahead. I could not bear to think otherwise. But as the minutes ticked away and no service station appeared, my positive attitude changed to fear that blended into the murky night around us.

Few cars passed and nothing surrounded us but God's world with a little asphalt underneath. I could not bear to look at the gauge, yet kept glancing at the needle as it crept toward the place it must not pass. At 2 A.M., my stomach started to churn and my shoulders grew knots. The needle had passed the halfway mark. Dad's voice haunted me: "You will have no warning before you run out."

To calm the growing panic, I prayed. "Please God, help me find an open service station soon." The minutes dragged by. *Should I wake Ken? What can he do? How much longer do we have? What if we run out of gas and there is no safe place to get off the road?* Trees lined both sides of the roadway. I tried to recall when I last saw a turnoff or a possible driveway to someone's house.

When the indicator hit the three-quarter mark, I quit looking. Occasionally luminous eyes peered out of the darkness as we rolled past the trees, but nothing else. No cars. No signs of human life anywhere.

An hour later, Ken stretched and peered outside. "Sure is dark. Where are we?"

"Somewhere in the mountains," I mumbled.

He looked at the dashboard. "Better get some gas."

"I can't. All the stations are closed."

"Closed?" Ken sat up straight and looked at the clock.

"But the gauge is . . ."

"I know, but there aren't any service stations open. When I saw the last one, we were nearly three-quarters full."

"Well, turn around and go back," Ken said.

"I can't. That was over three hours ago."

"Three hours!"

One of the children mumbled something, and everyone in the back shifted.

"Three hours?" Ken's voice dropped to a whisper. "The tank is nearly empty."

"I know."

Silence prevailed as I drove slowly into the darkness, praying with each turn of the wheel. *Please keep us safe and keep the children and Sandy sound asleep.* I felt nervous enough without having to hear, "Are we going to run out of gas?" every few minutes.

Finally, Ken said, "Stop here. I'll drive now."

As I stepped out and walked around the car, the cool night sent chills up my spine. When I opened the passenger door, an owl hooted in the distance. I jumped. Thankfully, the baby continued to sleep soundly when Ken handed him to me.

Slowly Ken wound his way through the darkness looking for some sign of life in case we needed help. No cell phones, no highway emergency call boxes existed at that time—only a long, dark, narrow highway winding up and down, curving through a forest.

Around four o'clock, Ken stopped the car. Although I did not sleep, my eyes stayed closed in pleading prayers. Gingerly, I opened them and looked at the gas

gauge that now pointed to E, yet the car was still running. Puzzled, I looked up. Ken pointed ahead.

BRIDGE OUT. The huge letters shot panic arrows
through my body. I looked around us—nothing but
deep, inky darkness. Was there room enough to turn
around and go back? If we did, where would we go?

Again, I looked at the gas gauge.

Still on empty.

Car still running, I breathed a prayer of thanks.

"Get the flashlight from the glove box," Ken whispered. "I'm going out to see what it looks like."

My heart jumped into my throat. What if he tumbled
and cracked his head on a rock? fell over a cliff? encountered a bear?

I tried calming my shaky hands as I handed him the
flashlight. *Please*, was the only prayer I could muster as
Ken and the flashlight quickly disappeared into the darkness. *Please . . . oh please, be with him . . . with us.*

I was about to scream his name when a bit of bob-
bing light emerged from the trees. As Ken drew near I
saw his smile and breathed a sigh of relief.

There is a temporary bridge right over that way." He
pointed. "The road is dirt, but it's safe."

We crossed over the gorge in safety and kept on
going. And going. And going. Neither of us said a word.
Quiet breathing prevailed from the backseat.

At 5 A.M., the gauge needle still held tight on empty,

and we were still going. Another hour passed as the wheels kept turning. My prayers went from pleading to *Thank You, oh thank You, thank You.* With every mile, our amazement grew.

A little before six in the morning, with the sky just beginning to lighten, we drove into a small town.

One single traffic light.

Turned red.

We stopped and a police car drove alongside us. I rolled down the window. The officer rolled down his.

"Where's the nearest gas station?"

"Just around the corner, to your left. He'll be open in a few minutes."

"Thanks," I said. Tears of relief and thanksgiving welled up.

"Have a nice day," said the officer as the light turned green.

Ken turned the corner and pulled up to the pump.

The engine died.

"Are we there yet?" floated up from the back.

My heart sang, "Oh yes, we're here. Thanks, God. We're here . . . all safe."

CHAPTER 3

Touches from Heaven

My body and my mind may become weak, but God is my strength. He is mine forever (Psalm 73:26 NCV).

When life's storms are raging all around, isn't it comforting to know someone is close-by—close enough to touch? Someone to hold your hand, someone with whom to pray, someone to calm and protect you. You can be assured that God is always there in the midst of the storm. He'll never leave you alone; He'll walk beside you through the storm and lead you safely home.

A Burgundy Valentine

DONNA ARLYNN FRISINGER

This was ridiculous. Of course the local dime store wasn't going to carry burgundy leotards. But I was desperate. I needed one, and I needed it fast!

As Rochester High School's dance team director, to thirty-some teenage girls, I was used to playing "Mom" and taking care of last-minute emergencies. Whether it was a missing button, replaced by the quick fix of a safety pin, picking up students who needed a ride, or running to retrieve a prop someone had left in the hallway right before it was time to perform, I prided myself on being able to handle any crisis they threw my way. Once or twice, I'd even been known to peel off my own T-shirt, pants, or shoes to give to some girl who'd *accidentally* forgotten hers at home.

But a burgundy leotard presented an impossible challenge. I'd ordered a bunch of them from a dance catalog months back, along with the matching tights. One of the mothers had volunteered to make cute pink wrap-around circle skirts to complete their outfits for a Valentine basketball halftime show, and we were only two hours away from tipoff.

93

Sophomore Pam Zimmerman had come charging down the school hallway, in a panic earlier that day. "Mrs. Frisinger! I can't find my burgundy bodysuit! I've looked everywhere for it!"

"*Everywhere?*" I asked. I knew these girls. They were forever losing things—or claiming someone else had taken something because "I left it right here!"

"Everywhere!" Pam bellowed. "Even under my bed! What am I gonna do, Mrs. Frisinger?" Ever the drama queen, now she was in tears close to hyperventilating.

"Calm down, Pam," I confidently reassured her. "One of the other girls probably just picked it up by mistake. It'll show up. We'll ask at practice."

But practice had come and gone, and still no burgundy leotard. Which was why I now found myself at the town's only department store frantically scanning the underwear aisles in search of the impossible. I'd just located a small pile of black leotards and was frantically digging through them.

"May I help you?" The salesclerk had apparently noticed my rummaging and, in order to keep me from entirely destroying her tidy display, figured she might want to help me out, I supposed.

"Yes," I answered. "I'm looking for a burgundy leotard."

"I'm sorry," she said, straightening the pile even as we spoke. "All we have is black. We've never carried any other color."

"I know," I answered. "I was just hoping."

"Well, hope all you want. But you're not going to find a burgundy bodysuit here." She smiled weakly and hurried off to take care of a more prevalent problem at the sound of a loud crash, followed by the scream of a howling toddler.

I bowed my head to pray. *"Lord, I know this is really not a very important issue in the big scheme of things going on the world today. But You know I really need a burgundy leotard, and I need it now! If I don't come up with one, Pam won't be able to perform tonight and all of our formations will be really messed up. We've all worked so hard on this special Valentine show. You are the God of impossibilities. Could You please provide me with the* impossible?"

I finished with a sigh. I'd done everything humanly possible to come up with a bodysuit. I'd checked the lost-and-found, called every mother, scoured the dressing room, combed through lockers, and pleaded with girls. Now I opened my eyes and started to walk away.

But wait! What is that? There, sticking out from underneath the counter, on the floor, was a scant smidgen of something—burgundy. *It couldn't be . . . could it?*

As I reached down to pull out the piece of cloth, my heart was pounding. Now, as I stood up, it skipped a beat, to then pitter-pat in a fresh cadence of joy. I couldn't believe my eyes! It was a burgundy leotard. It was a size medium, too, just what I needed! I hadn't even thought to tell God I needed it in a medium!

I shrieked and then started to laugh—loudly—hooting

and giggling hysterically. The sales woman came rushing back to my side. "What's wrong? Are you okay?"

Now I was doubled over, tears spilling down my cheeks. I raised my arm to reveal the burgundy bodysuit.

"Bu . . . bu . . . but we don't carry burgundy body-suits!" she exlaimed in disbelief.

"I know! I know! But God does!" She looked at me like I was crazy. I was. Crazy in love with a God so con-cerned about my piddley little needs that He'd sent an angel, to drop off a medium-size burgundy bodysuit right where I could see it!

"I'll take it," I said, as I handed her the leotard. "Please hurry. I've got to get to the game!"

Racing into the band room, I found my squad already dressed and stretching out. Pam stood to one side in tears, dejected. She had on her black leotard in hopes I might let her perform that way. "Pam, you know I can't let you do that," I said. "You'd really stick out . . ."

"I know," she said sniffling. "I was just hoping, and so were the girls . . ."

"*But, I can* let you perform in this!" I said, cutting her off, as I plucked the burgundy leotard from the sack I was carrying.

Her eyes bugged out and her mouth dropped open.

"Oh, Mrs. Frisinger!" one of the other girls yelled. "You found Pam's bodysuit!" Everyone applauded now, yelling and squealing, as they jumped up and down.

I raised my hand. "No, it wasn't me, girls. But *God* had one special-delivered to Rochester, Indiana, tonight." I handed Pam the leotard. "Well, don't just stand there. Get changed!"

The dance team did an awesome job that evening. I was proud of them. And as they reached their finale—a heart formation—I caught Pam's eye to wink. The smile plastered across her face reached the rafters.

Now, I grinned up to heaven. "Happy Valentine's Day, Lord," I said. "I'll never forget Your special valentine to me today. You are just way too cool!"

A Friend for Room 4

JEANNINE HUBBARD

The bell rang and my fifth-grade students leapt to their feet. They grabbed their backpacks and shoved past one another toward the door. "Don't push," I called after them. It was useless. In my twenty-two years of teaching I'd never come across a class of kids as rowdy and impossible to reach as this one.

The students who filed into room 4 of Hall District School in Las Lomas, California, each day came from such varied backgrounds. Some were in an English-speaking classroom for the first time. Many carried around anger, fear, or frustration about problems at home, which they often took out on one another. Any activity I dreamed up, from painting a mural to performing a folk dance, inevitably ended in an argument. How would we ever get through the whole school year when things were already this bad just a month into it?

That evening at home I graded what few assignments had been turned in. As soon as I finished, I picked up the newspaper, eager to distract myself. Nothing caught my eye, so I got into bed. My thoughts returned to my students. With all my years of experience, why couldn't I get through to them? I'd tried every new teaching method I heard about. *Lord, I'm at my wit's end. Please send a miracle to room 4.* Exhausted, I sank quickly into sleep.

I awoke with a start. It was 3:30 A.M. Something had flashed through my mind—something from the newspaper —but I'd lost what it was. I turned on my lamp and flipped through the paper. My attention was drawn to the letters to the editor. One in particular caught my eye. It was written by an elderly woman who wanted to thank a little girl she had seen at a fast-food restaurant. They had smiled at each other, then the child stopped to give her a kiss on the cheek. The woman, Mrs. Elizabeth Jarboe, wanted to share how much that small gesture had meant to her.

I clipped the letter and tucked it in my bag, then went back to bed.

The next school day started typically. I was handed more pink citation slips than homework assignments by my students. Two kids had been fighting on the bus, another had been accused of stealing lunch money, and still another was sobbing and wouldn't tell me why.

It took a good ten minutes just to get them all to settle down. Finally I pulled the newspaper clipping out of my bag. "We talk lots about how negative actions have negative effects," I said. "Today, I want to show you how positive actions have positive effects." I began reading Mrs.

Jarboe's letter aloud. Halfway through, I noticed that the classroom had become silent. There was no scuffling, no whispering, no fidgeting. I glanced up and saw something I hadn't seen yet that school year: my students were giving me their undivided attention. "I hope it made that little girl happy to be able to express such a loving impulse, and I wish she could know it made me very happy," the letter finished.

I looked up. "Mrs. Jarboe has lots to handle at home," I told the kids. "Her husband has health problems and she works hard to take care of him. She is going through a sad time. Do you see why it meant so much to her for that little girl to give her a kiss?"

There was a pause. Then a hand went up . . . "My great-grandma is sick. I help take care of her too."

Another hand . . . "My father died last year and my mom doesn't know how we're going to pay our bills."

And another . . . "My brother got arrested for taking drugs."

Usually I had a tough time getting any information at all from them. Now it seemed everyone wanted to talk.

"There were gunshots by my house, and now I can't play outside anymore."

Even more amazing than hearing the kids tell about their problems was the way the other students responded—not with taunts or snickers, but with looks of sympathy and understanding.

"Let's write to Mrs. Jarboe. That'll cheer her up," one student suggested. The rest of the class agreed.

"That's a great idea," I said. "Anyone who wants to can write to her, but we can't expect her to write back. She has enough to do already." The bell rang and my students got up and moved toward the door—with almost no pushing. I went home feeling encouraged. *Please, God, let this be a turning point.*

The next morning, I walked into room 4 to find my desk heaped with letters, cards, drawings, and photographs—all addressed to Mrs. Jarboe. As the kids settled into their seats, I shuffled through the pile. I'd never managed to get even half the students to hand in a homework assignment, yet all thirty-four of them had turned in something to send Mrs. Jarboe. For some, it was their first letter in English! My class was much calmer that day. Over the next few weeks, the kids continued to be more open. They started treating each other with respect, thanks in large part to that letter in the newspaper.

I thought that was the end of it, until one day when I found an enormous envelope stuffed in my school mailbox. It was from Mrs. Jarboe! My students' faces lit up when they saw that huge envelope on my desk. Had Mrs. Jarboe sent a gift of some kind? I opened it and pulled out a letter. Then another, and another. Each was addressed to a different student. She answered every one of their letters individually! "There's one for all of you!"

I said, passing out the letters. I watched their faces as they read. Moving between the rows of desks, I read over their shoulders. Mrs. Jarboe had asked about their lives, encouraging them to share their problems with her—and she promised to write back.

My students could hardly wait to reply to their new pen pal. We established a rule that if the kids wanted to keep their letters private, they would seal them. If they wanted me to read them out loud, they wouldn't. Most left them unsealed, so I got to know my students along with Mrs. Jarboe. There was something on my desk either to, or from, Mrs. Jarboe practically every day. They trusted her to take their problems, big or small, seriously. Schoolyard bullies, sibling rivalry, bad grades—no matter what the trouble, she helped put things in perspective— for me as well as my students.

Every holiday became an opportunity for the kids to make cards and decorations for their beloved Mrs. Jarboe. Copies of A papers were sent to her. At the end of the year I videotaped the class performing the folk dance they never could cooperate enough to do and sent the tape to Mrs. Jarboe. I'd been trying so hard to get through to my students using new teaching methods and group activities. Mrs. Jarboe showed me what they really needed was much more simple: to feel loved and appre- ciated as the special, unique individuals God had made them.

Mrs. Jarboe didn't stop with those kids. For the next ten years she was a faithful correspondent and confidante to the students of each new class in room 4. My students bestowed on her hundreds of valentines and Christmas cards, as well as their deepest hopes and dreams. Even as her eyesight began to fail and her handwriting got shakier, Mrs. Jarboe kept answering every letter individually. By the time I retired in 1996, Mrs. Jarboe had touched the lives of 370 of my students. I met Mrs. Jarboe only once, when she came to visit one of my classes, but she was the best teacher's aide I could have ever hoped for!

In 1997 Mrs. Jarboe passed on, and her daughter gave me a box overflowing with letters, photos, and artwork from my students. "Positive actions have positive effects," I'd told the kids. And here was the proof.

I'd asked God one difficult night to send a miracle to room 4. Never could I have guessed the form that miracle would take—that a child's kiss would bring us Mrs. Jarboe.

The First Day

JOHNIE ROBBINS

For the past two years, it seems I've done little other than take up space. So I decided I should get out and do something constructive. A recent newspaper article mentioned the growing need for substitute teachers. I figured I could do that—I'd be doing the schools a favor and earning extra cash at the same time.

I get my first call at 5:30 on a Monday morning. I'm informed that I am to teach fifth grade at a school across town. I jump out of bed, go into the kitchen, and start a pot of coffee. Dressing takes longer than expected, but a last check in the mirror tells me that, for an "old gal," I look pretty good. I grab a couple muffins and put them on a napkin, pour coffee into a thermal car mug, and head out the door.

As I drive down the highway, the realization of what I'm doing hits me like a box of math books flying through the windshield. This is the stupidest thing I've ever done. I've never taught school before! I can keep four grandkids busy, but what am I going to do with a room full of eleven-year-olds?

Well, it's too late to back out now. I have to go through with this. I begin to pray. My talk with God doesn't mention anything I'm thankful for or anything remotely concerned with anyone but me. *Please Lord, I need help and I need it now. Stay with me on this.* Suddenly I can hardly breathe. I want to turn the car around and go home and hide, but those kids are depending on me. *Why did I think I could do this? What will my friends think when they hear I was laughed out of the classroom?*

When I reach the school, I nibble on a muffin and sit in my car while I finish drinking my coffee. I tell myself again that this is what I should be doing, but I don't believe a word I say. Every time I think, *I can do it,* the thought hits me, *And just what makes you think that?*

At the school door, I straighten my shoulders, hold my chin up, and paste a smile on my face. If I'm lucky and look like I know what I'm doing, maybe no one will be able to tell that I'm clueless.

I take a deep breath and step into the office. After checking out the staff and teachers, I decide that, though I'm a little older, I at least look the part.

A staff member greets me warmly and introduces me to a teacher who takes me to my classroom. She says that today both of us will be giving evaluation tests and that she will be next door if I need help. I assure her that I'll call if I need assistance, but at the same time I wonder how soon I can yell "help!" without looking like I was hired straight from panic city.

I open the substitute's folder on the teacher's desk and find that the first thing I'm supposed to do is check attendance and take lunch count. How do I do that? I check through the rest of the folder. Information is given on fire drills, tornado drills, and what to do if a suspicious person is seen in the building. *Please Lord*, I pray silently, *if any of those things happen, just let me drop dead.* Finally I find a paper on which to put the lunch count. Maybe some kid will help me check attendance.

I greet the children and write my name on the board. Bless them, they are eager to help, and I find it's not necessary to call upon the teacher next door for two hours and thirteen minutes. My morning goes surprisingly well, although I find myself continually praying, *Please God, stay with me here; help me out on this.* Still, I'm sure God has more important things to do than watch over a nervous substitute teacher.

Lunch in the teacher's lounge makes me feel old. Most of the teachers are younger than my kids. For crying out loud, I'm the age of their grandparents! It's been so long since I carried on a conversation about burping babies and diaper rash, if I open my mouth the others will think I'm from a different planet.

After lunch, I go to the teacher's restroom, where in the mirror I see wrinkles I'm sure were not there this morning. *At the rate I'm going, I'll look like I'm 110 years old by 2:00.* It's a pleasure getting back to the safety of my own classroom, where I continue giving tests.

An hour before school lets out, I'm told that when the students are finished with their work, I should let them draw. I pass out blank sheets of paper. At the end of the day, while we're straightening up the room, a student hands me a folded piece of paper and motions for me to bend down. When I do, she whispers, "This is kind of special because I've never made a card for a teacher before."

On the front is a border of flowers with my name in the center. Unexpected tears well up in my eyes. *Please God, don't let me cry—she thinks I'm a teacher.* I swallow and return her whisper: "This is special for me, too, because I've never taught before—so this is my first card."

She looks relieved. I put my arm around her shoulders and give her a hug as we exchange smiles. The bell rings, and I lay the unopened card on my desk. I then make sure that the children leave the school safely. Returning to my room, I sit down to write the regular teacher a note explaining what we've done during the day. The card catches my attention, and with a sigh, glad that the day is over and that I haven't made a complete fool of myself, I open it. Inside on the left are the words "God loves you" embellished with hearts and flowers, while on the right side is a big red heart.

Suddenly I realize that God wasn't too busy with other things today to keep an eye on me. He did stay with me. He helped me out. And his way of letting me know was through the little girl and her handmade card.

I sign out in the office, then start my drive home. In the car, I say one more prayer: *Thank You. My first day wasn't so bad after all.*

A Kiss from My Heavenly Daddy

HOLLY BAXLEY

Aren't you glad to be living back in your hometown?" my friend gently asked. I glanced down at
the ice cubes that were swirling around in my sweet ice
tea, unable to look at the concern on my friend's face.

How could I tell her that my heart grieved sometimes
as I drove down the road? So many landmarks reminding
me of a bittersweet past, of precious memories that were
fading too quickly, and the aches that refused to go away.

As an unbidden tear slips down my cheek, I brush it
away quickly hoping she wouldn't notice. She did. Compassion laced her features as she reached for my hand
and gave it a soft squeeze. "Well," she replies in her soft
southern drawl, "I'm glad you're here and that God put
you in my path." I feel a wobbly smile forming on my lips
and a well of thanks forming in my heart. But rather than
opening my heart and risking further exposure, I quickly
changed the subject, and we were on our way back to
lighthearted ground. We laughed about our children's

antics, commiserated over our failure as preschool mothers to keep our sanity, and savored the wonderful roasted chicken that came with a fruit garnish and poppy seed dressing.

But after lunch was over and we said our good-byes, I glanced back at the combined tea room and gift shop as a sweet memory from twenty years ago filled my mind. At a table draped in a white tablecloth and tulle, my mother, sister, and best friends were beaming brightly as they tempted their palates with various scrumptious cheesecakes. I could still smell the mint chocolate "grasshopper" cheesecake that I had chosen for my own that day. My wedding day was quickly approaching, and this was my mother's gift to my bridesmaids and me. That day seemed so surreal in so many ways, I remembered thinking. Soon I will be leaving home and starting a new life with my husband.

And as that thought crossed my mind, instantly I was back in the present, for that memory was combined with the painful reminder that I was living back in my hometown now, without my mother. It, too, felt very surreal.

I attempted not to think of her as I drove home to my husband and children. But I simply could not help myself. I passed the library where, as a young girl, she would take me to read. I'd turn the corner and see one of her favorite restaurants that she'd take me to on special occasions. A little further down the road, her former office where she worked as an office manager.

No matter how I tried to tell my heart not to think about her, it would rebel and constantly bring her courageous heart and spirit to my mind. And, inevitably, I would relive those last moments that I spent with her before she passed away and would examine each one with careful scrutiny. And this drive home was no different.

I tried to quiet myself and think only of my "to do" list for the rest of the day. Then a signal light changed from green to red, and as I glanced upward, I caught the sight of an airplane high in the sky heading off to some unknown destination. And my mind began to wander.

In the haze of the distant past, I could see an airplane boarding pass in my hand. A sweet anonymous donor paid for me to go home and see Mom one last time, for we had been separated by two states while my husband studied in seminary and I worked full time. Mom could no longer work; her debilitating disease had taken its toll. And my sister had sacrificed her own heart by choosing to take care of our Mom in our grandmother's home while her own immediate family continued to live two hours away.

Being able to be with Mom was such a relief to both myself and my sister. She took the desperately needed break to head back to her husband and two small sons, resting from the constant weariness of this slow and painful death.

As much as I endeavored to prepare my mind to see Mom in this state, it was still a shock. I could see her lying in a bed that seemed much too large for her petite frame. Weak and almost gaunt beyond recognition, the colon cancer wreacked havoc in its long war on her body. However, in spite of her obviously fragile condition, her spirit was as strong as ever.

She reveled in the details of seminary life and what it was like for me to live and work in such a big city. We talked of everything and nothing. She slept a lot and I watched her. I dozed off and woke to her watching me. When I couldn't take the heartache of looking at her, she graciously let me slip off into the living room to escape into a romantic comedy. She loved me, hugged me, prayed for me and did what she always did with me; mothered me.

The last night came for me to be with her. She was looking at me, and we both knew that it was "time." Time to burn whatever bridges needed to be burned, say what needed to be said, repair anything that needed mending. However, as we talked, we realized that she had been mending fences and burning bridges all our lives. She lived such a life of transparency that there just wasn't any water under the bridge to deal with. And I loved her even more dearly on that precious day of discovery. She always had such an unwavering faith in God that only grew as the time drew closer to leave this world and be with Him.

There was only one iota of small doubt in her normally unshakable faith. As she reaffirmed her deep love for me, she lamented that there wouldn't be anyone to love my sister and me the way that she does—with unconditional love that will just go and fight for our cause and lift us up and tenderly kiss the fears away. She wondered out loud if there was a way for God to remind us of her love. Would He do something so that we could know that she still thought of us and loved us, even from beyond the grave?

With tears streaming down my face, I could not answer that question. And it hurt so deeply to see doubt cloud her heart. I could only hug her and whisper, "I know you love me, Mom. I know and I won't forget."

Later I learned that my sister and my mom had a long talk after I left about what it meant to go on living after my mom passed away. My sister told her that God loves us so much that He sends kisses from heaven so that we know just how much we are loved personally and unconditionally. It gave my mom so much comfort that she made sure my sister passed it along to me. She called it "kisses from our heavenly Daddy."

Though I admit that in my grief, all these years later I had buried this thought in the deepest recesses of my heart. I lived far away from my hometown and even my state for many years, and not only was my mom physically buried, but I buried her in my heart, somewhere very deep, where memories could not clamor for attention and grief would be abated.

But returning to my hometown? It was as if my heart exhumed all the feelings I thought had died in me and breathed new life into them. And now . . . now I saw her everywhere and in everything and in the everyday. And I mourned, for she never got to witness the deepening, maturing love of my marriage, nor met her wonderful grandbabies that miraculously completed my husband's and my life when they were adopted and placed in our arms. She would have loved them so, and they her. I know she would have spoiled them in a way that only a grandmother can.

At first, it was distressing to think of the memories and the loss, and then somehow, slowly over time, the memories became comforting, yet no less painful. But even in that, I could feel the healing that was taking place in my heart. Trading my sorrowful memories for the delighted ones and the laughter she brought in my life. Or on a day like this one, where I visited the tea-room, mixing new memories with the nostalgic. And for me, that was enough.

The next thing I knew, I was pulling up in my drive-way, not even remembering the drive home. Silently I breathed a prayer of thankfulness for God's protection. I've got to stop doing this, I fussed at myself. And life went on that day.

But what happened the following morning, I never envisioned.

After getting ready for work, I was summoned into my four-year-old daughter's bedroom at her request. As I followed her in, I noticed she had the contents of all her play jewelry on her bed. She fingered them for a moment and then cried, "This one!" and triumphantly held up a gold necklace that she had gotten for a Christmas present. As she lifted it higher she frowned.

"Wait one minute, Mama."

With those words she turned back to the strewn treasure of spangles and beads. "Yesssssss!" she gleefully chortled as her fingers closed around a small "golden" ring. She slipped it on the necklace, like a charm, and then demanded, "Sit down."

As I sat on the edge of her bed, I felt her slip the necklace with it's newly found charm around my neck. "I can't see, Mama. Lower." I crouched down lower and lowered my neck further. I heard a snap and then the words, "Got it."

She looked at me with love and said, "You look really pretty, Mama! Do you like it?"

Like it?

What she didn't realize is that the very necklace she slipped around my neck once belonged to my own beautiful mama. My sister had lovingly made my daughter some costume jewelry out of Mom's own jewelry collection. And now . . .

Now Mom's necklace is around my neck. One I had watched her put on many times on her way to her work.

One she fingered and toyed with as she would tell me of her latest revelation from reading the Bible.

No one told my daughter to do this. We hadn't even talked about jewelry for the day. She knew I usually grabbed something to somewhat match what I'm wearing, and sometimes she wore her own pretty jewelry to preschool.

Even more puzzling to me is that the play ring "charm" looks a lot like my mom's high school class ring. A golden ring, with an oval ruby inset.

I fingered it all with wonder and tried not to let the tears fall. I hugged my precious daughter and choked a "thank you" to her. Unaware of how priceless this treasured gift was, she skipped off down the hall, pleased with making her mama happy. As I took one last look in the mirror before we left for school and work that morning, I looked at my mother's necklace in the mirror, and her eyes staring out from my own.

And yes, I wore it to work. Some may have wondered about the costume play ring for the charm, but let them wonder.

It's not just a necklace. It is both a symbol of love from my daughter who wanted to share . . . and a kiss from my heavenly Daddy. A message sent from heaven, just for me.

Thank you, Mom. I love you so much and miss you too.

What Am I Doing Here?

BETTY GOFF

When the wife of a local doctor spoke to our Ladies Auxiliary several years ago, she stirred us with the need for volunteer aides at our overcrowded county hospital.

As a mother of four, I felt at first that this challenge didn't relate to me. But then in all honesty I admitted to myself that with my children in school I did have the time. There was something else, too, that, deep down, prodded me into some kind of activity where I might give more of myself.

I signed up for the necessary courses in hospital routine, and in six weeks I was a full-fledged hospital volunteer, pink uniform and all.

On my first assignment I was introduced to Peg, the senior aide. Peg was a woman of about forty-five with years of experience in her field. Looking me over rather dubiously, she said, "Come on, let's get to the P.M. care." With my twelve hours of training fresh in mind, I knew this meant changing beds and washing the patients.

We collected the necessary sheets, pillowcases, towels and so on, put them on our little cart and set off for our first patient. Only then did I find out this floor was for patients with terminal cancer.

The first patient was an elderly man. The stench in the room was unbearable and I fought the waves of nausea that threatened to overcome me. Peg and I each took one side of the bed and lowered the safety bars. Peg unceremoniously pulled the covers off the patient, removed his johnny coat and proceeded with her job of washing. Then, to my distress, she realized that she had forgotten some piece of equipment and quickly left the room, instructing me to stay put and be sure the patient didn't fall out of bed.

There I was, forced to keep my eyes on this man who looked like a living skeleton lying on his bed.

What am I doing here? I thought. My head whirled and I was sure I would faint any second. I tried to keep my mind on something, anything except this shriveled piece of humanity. Finally, Peg came back and together we changed the bed and left the room, only to face other patients just as frightening.

When it was time to go home the head nurse thanked me for coming, and Peg asked if I would be back. I assured her I would, but I wasn't so sure that I could.

For the next few days I could think of little else but the misery I had witnessed. Why not quit? But I couldn't reconcile myself to giving it up. Others did the same work. Were they so hardened to suffering?

I prayed for an answer and it came. It was so simple and was actually what had motivated me to volunteer for this work in the beginning, though I didn't know it at the time. I realized that whether I was there to see it or not, people were suffering and dying. My not seeing it did not make it unreal. But if I could, by my presence, reassure one patient just a little or give some small service that the regular staff was too busy to give, that patient would be better off than had I stayed home in my own agreeable world.

So I went back to the hospital. A few weeks later I met a little lady well into her seventies who was in the very last stages of cancer. She was delirious and I heard her pathetic call for "Mama." I went to her bedside and took her gnarled old hand in mine.

"It's all right, dear, I'm here," I reassured her, gently stroking her hand. Shortly afterward she died in a contented sleep.

On another occasion, as I was leaving for home, one of the women called out as she saw me pass her door. I went in to see what she wanted.

"I hate to bother the nurse," she said. "Would you do me a favor?" Gingerly and with step-by-step instructions from the patient I scrubbed her dental plates and returned them to her intact.

And so it went. No life-saving miracles, just little everyday services. The small gesture to make one human being feel better for a while.

Recently, I took time off from my volunteer work to have baby number five. But I will go back to the hospital when I can. For I have learned one sure way to get closer to God, as promised in the Book: "As ye have done it unto one of . . . these . . . ye have done it unto me" (Matthew 25:40 KJV).

The Crumpled Yellow Note

VICKI P. GRAHAM

I was barreling up the highway headed for the Interstate in a rush to get to the Oklahoma City University trauma center to be with my client of eighteen years who lay in a coma. The doctors reported she would not live till morning, and I didn't want her to die alone. As I sped by our church, which lay just outside of town, I saw a friend standing at the side of the highway frantically waving a yellow piece of paper trying to get me to stop.

My first thoughts were, *How did Judy know I'd be coming this way and why was she trying to stop me?* No one knew of my mission. As soon as I got the hospital call I had jumped in my car and sped off.

I wheeled into the church parking lot and screeched to a stop. Judy flung the door open, pushed the yellow paper in my hand, and said, "God just told me to write this to you. I don't know what it means. Do what it says!"

Puzzled, I tore out to the highway. Nobody should

try driving over seventy, unfolding a paper, and reading it, but I couldn't wait. The note said, "Vicki, God said you must get to your friend's side, lay hands on her, and anoint her with oil. But He said you *must* find a prayer partner! There is power in the prayer of two."

What to do? I fretted as I read the note again. I knew no one at the Oklahoma City hospital, and time was of the essence. I began praying—for my friend, for God to heal her, for Him to provide a strong believing prayer partner ready to go to war.

The words rolled out of my mouth as the two hundred miles rolled away beneath my tires. By the time I slammed into the trauma center parking lot, I was sure God had a miracle waiting. Racing into the ICU, I located the information desk, secured the room number, and raced down the hall. Had I been racing for hours?

It all came to a screeching halt when I turned into my friend's room, and there was a young man kneeling at her bedside. He was holding her poor yellowed hand, and in his other hand he held a vial of oil.

"Who are you?" I gasped.

"I'm your client's brother," he replied. "We haven't spoken to each other in years. I live in Missouri now and pastor a church there. In my prayers this morning, the Lord clearly told me to get to Oklahoma City University Hospital to pray for my sister's life. And," he went on, "He promised me there would be a prayer partner to join me in battle. Would that be you?"

I tearfully handed him the scrunched-up yellow note. The look on his face was joy and hope. We went to work prayerfully to obey the Father's will, especially since He had so lovingly already prepared the way for us! We would not be denied the sparing of my friend's life and soul.

Two weeks later, she was off the dialysis machine and headed home in the ambulance with her long-lost brother by her side. As for me? I just love to tell the stories of God's miracles.

The Ultimate Realtor

PAMELA R. WATTS

My husband's company is famous (some might say, "notorious!") for promoting its associates by way of relocating them. When we first experienced this, we were ecstatic. The opportunity for advancement, accompanied by a substantial pay raise, and the transfer to a desirable community seemed to leave nothing left to wish for. For the first time in my adult life, I would finally be able to move into my dream house. After years of living in an older home that needed far more improvements and repairs than we could possibly afford, at last I could realize my vision of a big, beautiful, brand new home that asked nothing of us other than we just enjoy it.

There was just one obstacle. After making our old home "show ready" with new carpet, landscaping, and so on, we couldn't seem to sell it. Months after our move to the new location, our former home was still on the market. In a desperate, futile effort we tried the old home-selling trick of burying a statue of the patron saint of lost causes upside-down in the front yard! It was at the same time when we learned that the new church we had joined had a prayer chain committed to lifting its members' needs in prayer. At our wits' end, we presented our concern to the prayer chain members, all the while hoping that we wouldn't appear ridiculous for requesting prayer for something as "frivolous" as a real estate transaction. (Looking back, I can't help but smile as I realize how spiritually young and ignorant we were in our understanding of the many uses of prayer!) Having already waited in vain for months for any interested buyers, let alone a firm offer, within just a few days of sharing our prayer request we received a promising offer, and it wasn't long before the sale of our house was complete.

We were dumbfounded by this new encounter with the awesome power of prayer. It wasn't long, though, before it became our habit to cover more and more challenges and decisions in prayer, which was soon to serve us well. Once again Brent was forced to contend with another job change and relocation, only this time we were devastated. We loved our home, our church, our community, and our proximity to family and many dear friends. What on earth could God possibly need with us in Waco, Texas, anyway? Unlike our first move, which had been quick, decisive, and joyful, this time the process was slow, uncertain, and agonizing. For months we waited, watched, and prayed for the outcome, all the while rebelling against this unwelcome change in our future. Brent contacted every headhunter and job search resource at his disposal in order to find another job that would keep us where we wanted to be, but without success.

As the weeks went by, the likelihood that we would have to move became increasingly clear. Finally yielding to the inevitable, we began to contact Realtors in the Waco area. Through a Realtor friend we were referred to a precious woman who patiently showed us home after home in a variety of neighborhoods. We were still uncertain, waiting to see where "the cloud would move us," praying that we would find the right house, that the right doors would open. I found myself sharing this fact with our Realtor, when she confided in turn that she was praying for us as well. How I needed that added assurance just then! Together we searched in vain for a comparable home which would compensate me for the loss of my spacious, beautiful residence, and yet was also in our price range. I began to lose hope that such houses were to be found!

In desperation, Brent and I revisited a house that had initially intrigued us. We had seen this house on the market about six months earlier, when we had somewhat prematurely begun some house hunting. When we began to search in earnest, there it was, still for sale, with no other offers anywhere in sight. Let me first explain something about this house. It was the ugliest home we've ever considered! The fixtures were dated, the paint job was old, the carpet even older, and the whole place reeked of smoke. I thought it would have been a great candidate for a home-improvement reality show. Buying this house would be a decided leap of faith! However, I leaned on the help of the vision and imagination of our realtor and a decorator we even called in, and slowly began to see the home's potential—to view it not as what it was, but what it could be.

A final attribute of this house was that it was available through "a fire sale," in this case, a casualty of divorce. This one was especially bitter, messy, and ugly. So much hostility remained between the ex-husband and wife that the title company actually had to schedule two separate closings, because the two of them couldn't even be in the same room to sign the papers together. Since the house really needed a lot of work, our initial offer was low, about 10% under asking price. However, the husband (who was living in it and paying the mortgage) accepted it immediately. The wife was a different story. She flatly declined without proposing a counteroffer, and refused to negotiate with us any further. We started hearing some things that made us nervous: "She's depressed and having trouble making decisions; she's not from the United States originally and doesn't understand American real estate."

"Heavenly Father, what have we gotten into here? Are we walking onto real estate quicksand? Is this woman going to hold up negotiations just to exact revenge on her ex?"

We didn't know what the answer was, and we asked

our pastor to pray with us. Let me now confess that Brent and I can sometimes be a little overly enthusiastic in our pursuit of a bargain . . . okay, let's face it—we're cheap! "Is our offer too low? Are we being unfair? Is this a sign of a closed door, and we should just walk away?" Having seen loved ones try to put divorce behind them while still bound together by real estate, I've witnessed the struggle and frustration of trying to move on yet still remaining tied to the past. I found myself feeling compassion for this broken family. I prayed for them to experience resolution and healing. I trusted that we could still find another house, but I worried about what would become of this family if we were to withdraw. We were the only offer they'd had in seven months.

Raising our bid or walking away were two alternatives we could choose. However, for us to purchase the house at our price meant that the ex-wife would have to have a change of heart. That option was a matter for the work of the Holy Spirit, so we began to pray that God would change her heart. It was the only other way the situation could go forward, and was something only He could do. A few days later, our Realtor, who'd been out of town, called me and said, "Pam—it's a miracle. She's accepted your offer as it stands." We received everything we asked for with no changes to our contract.

At the same time, we still had to contend with the sale of our current home. As hard as it can be to find a new house, it can be even harder to sell the old one! Should we put it on the market? If we sold too soon, we could find ourselves temporarily homeless. Too late, and we risked running into the same difficulties we had with our previous sale. I've always found that part of the enormous stress of moving is trying to coordinate precisely the timing of all these delicate transactions!

How could I know that God had not only picked out our future home, but had also already selected our future home buyers? When I first met Janet Ritchie in my son's preschool music class, we found we had much in common and decided to get together outside of class. I soon learned that her family was hoping to move into a larger home better suited to their needs, but she and her husband were discouraged by the rising prices in our community.

"Too bad you can't just buy my house!" I joked. My neighbors, concerned about us selling to "strangers" and upsetting the delicate balance of friendships in our tight-knit little cul-de-sac, would be so reassured. Like me, Janet was an outgoing, bubbly blonde Christian woman with a daughter and son precisely the ages of my own. If we sold our house to this family, our neighbors would never even notice that we left! At that moment, though, the timing wasn't quite right for them to be thinking seriously of buying (or for us to be thinking seriously of selling). We both laughed it off as one of those, "wouldn't be hilarious if . . ."

notions. However, by the time we had entered negotiations on our Waco home, "the cloud" had also moved for the Ritchies and their casual interest grew into a firm offer. It wasn't long before we had agreed on an equitable purchase arrangement that benefited both families. In the space of one weekend, Brent and I signed contracts for both the purchase of our new home and the sale of our old one.

Our search for a home had ended, but our journey was just beginning. Through the painstaking process of fixing up our new home for our arrival, God was there, and directed us to the right people to help us. Through the myriad details of relocating a young family to a brand new community where we knew not a soul, God was there, and prepared new friends and neighbors to welcome us.

Sure, we had to abandon our "big beautiful house," but we also left behind its equally large mortgage, taxes, insurance, and utility bills. As a result, our finances were liberated to the point that we have been able to invest significantly in the future of our children, our church, and other priorities. What's more, since the "big beautiful house" required nothing from me, I was able to give it nothing, and left feeling that I had been just a tenant instead of a homeowner. In our current home, through God's provision, we have been able to bestow again and again our love and care in the way of remodeling and other improvements. After we had made our first set of significant changes throughout the house and had settled in, I received a visit from a dear friend who commented, "Of all the houses I've ever seen you live in, this is definitely my favorite." Having known and loved me most of my life, this friend was immediately at ease in a house that I had so clearly made my own.

Through this move in which God clearly orchestrated everything down to the minutest detail, we have been not just transferred, but transformed! The thin threads which connect us to church, friends, and community have been woven by God to create the beautiful tapestry of our life. It has been in this place that He has provided people, teaching, and countless other resources to call and equip us as we added through international adoption our third child. It has been in this place that our family has come to know Him intimately, love Him passionately, and serve Him wholeheartedly. It has been in this place He has seen fit to keep us over the last seven years, through several more job changes and even potential relocations.

At this point, whenever any question arises as to whether we may move again, our family has learned to answer confidently, "When the cloud moves." And finally, whenever we encounter friends trying to buy or sell a home, we just refer them to the Ultimate Realtor!

Through Rain and Hail

PEGGY FREZON

Riding in the passenger seat, I tried to hide my clenched hands. My husband and I were headed back to New York from a visit to my mom's in Vermont, and a major storm was predicted. I'm a nervous traveler in the best of conditions. But in bad weather, forget about it. Living in the Northeast, I begrudgingly accept that a little rain—and snow and sleet—must fall. But that never helps my anxiousness when the roads are less than perfect.

"What's the matter?" Mike noticed me fidgeting uncomfortably.

"Oh, nothing." I tried to sound casual. Mike wasn't worried about a potential storm, so why was I? It was late summer, which cut my list of travel-related weather concerns considerably, but still I stressed over any deviation, even when I knew I shouldn't. Like the time with the windshield wipers.

Several years ago we had a car that was in need of some TLC. We couldn't drive when it was raining because the windshield wipers hadn't worked for months. The wiper motor sounded like it was trying to go; it hummed and groaned. But the wipers jerked up only a fraction of an inch and flopped back down again. My husband wasn't adept at car repairs, and we didn't have enough money yet to get them fixed. So we just drove the car on sunny days and hoped for good weather.

One day I had to go to the pharmacy to get some medicine for one of the kids. I had to go; there was no choice. I glanced out the window. It was getting dark and overcast. If I was going to get there and back before the rain hit, I'd have to act fast.

Mike watched the kids while I jumped into the car. Just about halfway there, sure enough, a light sprinkle began. *Maybe I can still beat the worst of it,* I thought. But as I grabbed what I needed, paid, and rushed back out the door, the rain was coming down in torrents. A glance at the angry skies told me the rain would probably be falling for a long time. I didn't think I could wait it out. I prayed, "Okay, God. Please either stop this rain, or make my wipers work. Either way's okay by me. Just please help me get home safely."

I got into the car, held my breath, and pulled the wiper lever. They didn't budge. Just the same old motor groan and imperceptible budge. And the rain wasn't letting up any, either. *So much for praying.*

Then I got an idea. I could move the wipers manually. If I stopped the car, got out, and pushed the wipers by hand, and did this every few yards, could I make it home? I didn't want to do anything dangerous, but I knew a back way with very little traffic. It would be safe to drive slowly on those roads.

I set off, and very quickly the rain built up on my windshield. I struggled to see past the rivulets trailing down the glass. But just as I was getting ready to pull over and manually wipe my windows, the far wiper swept over in the most unexpected and unnatural movement, clearing the rain away from the windshield! Just one motion, and then it stopped. I couldn't believe it!

I drove a little farther, carefully, and then, just as the rain was building up again . . . swoosh! The wiper did it again! Every time the rain began to obstruct my view, that wiper cleaned my window so I could see!

As I pulled into my driveway, I wondered why God hadn't made my wipers work the regular way, even fixed them for good. Or why not stop the rain until I got home? But I knew one thing. He had gotten me home safely.

But that was then. This drive, from Vermont back to New York, was a different story. I wasn't so confident God could get me through the longer haul. We had only a few hours left to go, through the Adirondack Mountains and south, but still I worried. Light rain wouldn't be a big issue now that we had a car with working wipers. But this storm was supposed to be a doozy.

I hadn't even been able to enjoy our visit with Mom

earlier. I'd rushed through lunch, not thinking about catching up on news or just being together. All I could concentrate on was the storm, and beating it out. I gave Mom a big hug and dashed to the car.

As we traveled along, I prayed. "God, please, just get us home before the storm hits." I searched the skies for gathering clouds. I listened intently for the wind to pick up or any other telltale signal of impending storm. Driving would surely be hazardous with blinding rain and flash flooding sweeping across the pavement.

But as we continued along, the skies remained clear. Maybe we were going to beat it out after all! Our route wound us through the higher elevation of the Adirondacks. Suddenly, we saw something totally shocking for August. A white powder on the sides of the road. Orbs of ice as big as Ping-Pong balls scattered all over the road.

"Hail!" said Mike.

I stared out the window, my eyes wide and my mouth hanging open. The pavement was dark and wet. Tree limbs were down. And shiny green leaves, blown off the trees, decorated the roadway. It was obvious that a mighty storm caused this damage.

It was also obvious that the storm had passed by. As we drove back down the other side of the mountains, our path was clear. We got home without a problem.

Later, relaxing in the living room, I thought of how

silly I'd been for worrying. True, we hadn't beaten the storm. We had come along behind it. It wasn't exactly what I had expected, or asked for, but the outcome was the same. God had directed our path until we were home safely.

Suddenly, I realized how amazing God was. Why had He put us behind the storm instead of in front of it? I don't know, but if we hadn't come along behind, I would have never seen the result of His power, nor His ability to get us through. Why hadn't He fixed my windshield wipers completely that other time, instead of making them work just now and then? I can't tell, but I know that day, and every day, He gives me just what I need. Not always anything more, but never any less.

CHAPTER 4

When You Least Expect It

Anyone who is having troubles should pray. . . . And the prayer that is said with faith will make the sick person well; the Lord will heal that person (James 5:13, 15 NCV).

God is full of surprises! He loves to touch our lives with His love and care in simple, subtle ways. He doesn't wait until there's some kind of disaster or life-threatening problem to make Himself available to us. He comes in good times too. So don't be surprised when you see evidence of His hand touching your life when you least expect it.

Caught in the Jackknife!

MARY HOLLINGSWORTH

While I was in college in arid West Texas, my parents were living in gorgeous Fayetteville, Arkansas, where they ministered to a church. At Christmas break I drove home for the two-week holiday to celebrate with my family and enjoy a few days of rest from the breakneck school routine.

Arkansas at Christmas is truly beautiful, especially when it's covered in glistening snow. The evergreen trees and rocky mountains are a perfect showcase for God's winter glory. And even though driving the curly mountain roads can be challenging, especially when it's rainy or snowy, the scenic views are often breathtaking and make the tedious journey worth the effort.

A good friend of mine, Sue Fleming, lived a few miles north of Fayetteville in Springdale where she had a public bookkeeping service in her home. In fact, at one time she had been my parents' next door neighbor until circumstances caused each of them to move.

Before I left school to come home, Sue called and asked me to work for her in her bookkeeping business while I was at home for the holidays. She was trying to do her year-end closings and wrap up her bookkeeping requirements for the year. I eagerly agreed, since paying for an expensive private Christian school required all the money my parents and I could muster. Besides, Sue and I always had a great time together, so I looked forward to days of laughter and productivity.

I arrived home on Friday afternoon and enjoyed a quiet but fun weekend with my folks. Then on Monday I got in my car and started the twenty-mile trek to Sue's house to go to work. It had been raining the night before, and the weather was extremely cold, but the skies had turned brilliant blue, and I could see for miles in every direction. So I was zipping along the two-lane highway through southern Fayetteville with the radio playing, singing my favorite oldies, and enjoying the ride, thinking about the fun times ahead.

The route to Sue's included a stretch of highway that was fairly narrow and ran uphill between the edge of a large lake on the right and the vertical side of a mountain on the left. The side of the mountain had literally been sliced off to make room for the roadway. And in typical Arkansas fashion in those days, the road had no shoulders. You were within three or four feet of the mountain and three or four feet of dropping off the other side into the lake. So there was very little maneuvering space to do anything but go straight ahead.

I was traveling about sixty yards behind an eighteen-wheel Wal-Mart truck going up the hill. In Arkansas, Wal-Mart trucks are everywhere, because their headquarters is there. We were about halfway to the top of the hill when the truck hit a slick place in the road and jackknifed. I immediately screeched to a halt, and the traffic behind me quickly followed suit.

Meanwhile, the huge truck cab had spun around to the left, forming a giant V with the trailer, and the entire mega truck had begun sliding back down the hill . . . straight toward me.

I jerked my head around looking for escape options. Mountain on the left, lake on the right, cars stacked up behind me, and an out-of-control truck in front of me. Nowhere to go! If the truck continued sliding, I would be caught in the V and crushed in my little Plymouth Valiant.

Oh, dear Lord! I thought. *Help me! Stop that truck!*

The fifty yards between that mass of sliding metal and my car had now dwindled to about thirty yards. I could see the truck driver fighting madly to get the truck under control. His airbrakes were screaming, and his giant tires were locked and smoking from the friction with the pavement as he continued to slide sideways and backward down the mountain, rushing closer and closer toward me and the drop-off into the lake.

"Oh, God, please stop that truck!" I yelled at the windshield. "Please stop him!"

I sat frozen in place out of sheer panic, not able to move, as now the truck was within twenty yards of my little car. *Should I stay in the car or jump out and try to run? What should I do, God?*

Suddenly, for no apparent reason, the massive truck ground to a stop, still in the V shape, not ten yards from my car. I was sitting right in the middle of the V with truck wrapped around me on both sides.

I laid my head on my white-knuckled hands gripping the steering wheel and whispered, "Thank You, God. Thank You!"

The truck driver just sat in his truck, breathing hard from the physical exertion of manhandling the giant rig. Then he slowly turned his head, his eyes widening as it registered with him how close he came to crushing me. He just shook his head and offered me a weak "Wow! That was close; I'm sorry" smile. Then he carefully straightened out the cab and trailer, and methodically shifting through his many gears, pulled away up the hill.

Once I got my heart started again, I took my foot off the brake and started up the hill after him, but this time I let him get about a hundred yards ahead of me before I followed.

Now, I don't know about you, but I'm a firm believer in asking God specifically for what I need and want. And I'm so glad that on that particular day I asked Him to stop that truck. God always answers prayers. Sometimes

He says yes; sometimes He says no; and sometimes He says wait. The miracle that day was that He answered, "Stop!" at just the right moment to save me from being caught in the jackknife.

Unburdened

BRENDA ERVIN

John, I'm going to pick up some birdseed," I called to my husband. I had to get out of the house. My husband was suffering from depression, and lately I had been overwhelmed by the burden of caring for him.

Driving to the store, I felt frazzled. *I have to be strong for John and the kids,* I thought. But at times I needed someone to lean on.

I bought a twenty-five-pound bag of birdseed and was barely able to load it into the cart. Outside in the parking lot I noticed the cart rails blocked the way to my car. Now what am I going to do? Even this simple errand was turning into an ordeal.

I was struggling with the bag when two large hands grabbed the other end and helped me lift it out of the cart. I looked up to see the kind face of an older man. He didn't say a word, but his eyes were filled with compassion. Together we carried the birdseed to my car and dropped it into the trunk. Slamming it shut, I turned to thank the man for his help, but he was gone.

On the drive home, I had to pull over. I wept the tears I had held back for so long. Then in the stillness I gave thanks to God for sending someone to share my load and for giving me the strength to go on.

Michelle and Miracle

LINDA K. WHITE

Time for us to pack up and go home, kids." My children, Sam and Michelle, and their friends and I had spent a full, beautiful June day at our nearby city park exploring and enjoying the wonders of nature. But as we made our way back to the car, Michelle, my youngest of six kids, lagged behind. She was upset at seeing duck eggs lying smashed in and around the lake that housed wild ducks, geese, and water creatures.

And then my very compassionate six-year-old found one solitary unbroken egg. "Mommy! Mommy! Look what I found! Can I save it, Mommy? Please let me take it home so no one can smash it. Please, Mommy?"

All of this came out seemingly in one breath as she gently scooped up that one solitary egg nestled beside the root of a pine tree and ran toward me. I half feared she would fall in her haste and this egg, too, would be shattered.

"Okay, you can keep the egg to save it from being smashed." No sooner were the words out of my mouth than I had a sense of what was going to come next.

"Mommy, I know there's a baby duck in this egg. I

just know it. What do I do to hatch it?" Her eyes pleaded with me while my mind began tallying up all the reasons why we were not going to try to hatch that egg.

"Michelle, I was raised on a farm. I know that this egg does not have a baby duck in it." I proceeded to go down a list of whys. "None of the smashed eggs we saw had any sign of being fertile. And, honey, only heaven knows how long that egg has lain there cold. Eggs for hatching have to be kept warm."

To which my sweet, trusting child replied very gently as she cuddled the egg to her bosom, "Mommy, I know there's a baby duck in this egg, and God is giving me the special pet I asked him for." There was a finality in her voice.

What was I to do? I'd taught my children that a loving God cares about each and every concern we have, be it big or small. I'd told them that when we go to Him in prayer, trusting, He hears us and begins giving the situation His personal, all-powerful attention. But I knew the facts about the egg.

"Michelle, you can take the egg home and keep it while we give this matter a little more consideration." Secretly I hoped she would forget about it.

"Thank you, Mommy. Oh, thank you. I'll keep it warm and no one can touch it because they might break it. How do I keep it warm?" I saw a wisp of tender, instinctive motherhood glowing in her eyes.

Dear Lord, help me to be the mother she needs right now, I prayed. *Don't let her be hurt.*

When we arrived home, Michelle went to her bedroom and reappeared with the egg wrapped securely in her thickest baby doll blanket, looking for a warm place for her egg. The dining room window seat caught her eye. She arranged her "baby" in the greatest ray of sunlight and then went outside to spread the news about the special pet God was giving her.

Within seconds, it seemed, our dining room was filled with neighborhood children. They were permitted to see the egg, but "please, no touching."

Three days and nights passed with the egg taken from the window seat only to nap with Michelle or sit beside her when she rested. She was determined to keep that egg warm, but all her efforts were failing, and she came to me on the third day very troubled.

"Mommy, my egg is still cold. Doesn't the mother duck sit on her egg to keep it warm?"

I knew what that meant. "Michelle you are too heavy to sit on the egg. It will surely break."

"Mommy, please pray with me that God will warm my egg. We have to pray together, remember?" She had zeroed in on what I did not want her to zero in on: me setting an example of faith for her. *God, why couldn't it just be Michelle's faith project? Why target me? I know the facts. There is no duckling in this egg, and quite frankly, I'm ready to throw it all out the window!*

Still, with all odds against her, my child needed a prayer warrior, and that was that! God, in His infinite wisdom, would handle this in the manner He saw best; I needn't worry. And with that settled, in my heart and mind we prayed. It was not an easy prayer for me.

But faith does not fear the odds. It measures them, I believe, then prays in God's will and goes into action trusting for the answer. Our action was a new home for the egg: a deep pan, a soft towel, and the oven, which had a slightly higher than usual pilot light.

At some time within the following week, in the still of evening and a house quieted by sleeping children, I stood in the soft moonlight of our tiny kitchen and reaffirmed my request to the Lord. I prayed with all my heart for my daughter and the many others who looked on and would be affected by the outcome of this project. I laid one hand on the stove top and raised the other toward heaven, hoping some power of God would us me as a conduit to flow life into that egg.

In the weeks that followed, "Is it a duck yet?" became a regular part of our day. That was also the daily inquiry from the neighborhood children. My younger brother came to visit and upon hearing of our faith venture with an egg, he chuckled and reminded me, "Mother ducks turn their eggs each day, remember, Mother Duck?"

So the egg was turned daily by me and the children. In fact, I'm sure it got turned more than once daily. If the

Lord really was growing a duckling in there, it was going to come out mighty dizzy!

At the very end of July, Michelle was spending Friday night with a friend. I was getting ready for a swimming party with my Christian singles group when Sam said, "Mom, don't forget to turn the egg."

As I opened the oven door, I almost braced myself for the odor of rot my reflexes told me would be occurring. After all, this egg had been in a semiwarm oven for more than a month. "No. I trust God, I trust God," I said.

Carefully I removed the pan from the oven and peeked at its contents as I turned the egg. "Oh, no! Lord, someone broke Michelle's egg." I said it so loudly that Sam came running from the front porch.

The egg was definitely cracked. I was heartsick; Sam was stunned. Who could have been so careless as to break the egg that had taken on so much importance in our lives? "Oh, God, how do I tell my baby?"

The egg rested gently in my hand. Sam and I examined the large crack in the shell, neither of us knowing what to say. A portion of the shell about the size of a dime was missing.

Then I saw it: a throbbing motion behind the membrance.

"Sam, look!"

The throbbing was coming from a tiny break inside the egg!

"Dear God in heaven, You did it! It's a baby duck!"

I will never forget the feeling that flooded through me and, I'm sure, through the kitchen and house. Heaven and earth touched! That's the best way I could describe it.

By the next afternoon the duckling was in a new box-home with soft bedding, a warm light, and the most gorgeous puff of golden-bronze feathers I had ever seen! We awaited Michelle.

When Michelle came home, we slowly ushered her into the dining room doorway. "What is it? Where's my surprise?" she asked eagerly. "Don't tell me, I know what it is!" Her sparkling eyes caught sight of the box on the window seat where she had first laid that solitary egg for warmth. She ever so softly picked up her baby duck and, smothering her nose in its radiant pinfeathers, whispered, "He did it, Mommy! God did it for me! I will name him Miracle."

Michelle and Miracle had lovely times together. The two of them were the talk of the neighborhood. He lived with us for several months, but we decided that it was not safe for him to remain in the city. Today Miracle lives with other ducks at a beautiful lake in the country, and Michelle visits him frequently.

Michelle's mustard seed faith touched the lives of her family, her friends, and the neighborhood children. But most of all it helped me to put my own faith into action.

Snow Angel

STEPHANIE TERRY

The weather in Oklahoma is anything but predictable. By the time I was a junior in college in Oklahoma City, I had experienced some rather interesting weather phenomena. But one occasion will remain with me forever.

It was early March. The temperatures were still too cool for spring, but trees had leafed out and spring bulbs were up and promising lovely blossoms soon. That's what I noticed when I entered the Learning Center early in the evening to do some studying.

About 10:30 P.M. my roommate appeared at my desk asking if I was ready to go back to the room. I still had thirty minutes before the center closed, but I told her I'd come on with her. She, however, was already bundled against the ever-present Oklahoma wind and was getting too warm for inside the building. So she said she'd start on down to the dorm area and meet me in our room. I couldn't have been five minutes behind her.

When I stepped out the door, however, I was not expecting to see a full-blown blizzard! There was even thunder and lightning with it! The snow was flying hori-

zontally, and I couldn't even make out the lights of the
dorms about a quarter of a mile away. In fact, nothing
looked familiar in the white night. This was my first
"whiteout"!

Now, keep in mind, this college was a medium-sized
one, and while you may not know every student by
name, you certainly recognized faces. And until curfew
you could see people nearly anywhere you looked on
campus. But that night, as I stood just under the building's overhang in the center of the campus, I didn't see
a soul. The wind was howling and blowing the snow
across the ground so it looked as if no one had ever
dared mess it up with footprints. It was eerie to be sure
and very noisy, but I needed to get to the dorm and
plunged ahead.

I had trouble knowing where the sidewalk was. I
stepped very carefully, feeling for the concrete firmness
under my foot. The wind was blowing so hard, that several times my next step was in the grass. I also had to be
cautious because between the Learning Center and the
dorms are two sets of concrete steps. I recognized the first
one by the exposed railing on the wheelchair ramp. The
steps were completely covered with snow and looked like
a smooth slope. I decided the best way was to go down
the hill on the grass. Then if I fell, I would have less
chance of being hurt. As I was preparing to do that, I was
startled by a voice calling out, "Wait!"

I turned and saw a fellow right behind me. He said, "Let me have your books, and you take my arm. Let's get off the sidewalk and go down on the grass." As I stepped off the sidewalk, the drifted snow was thigh-high on me. My wool skirt and coat were lying on top of the snow. The guy saw that and said loudly but ever so sympathetically, "Oh my, I bet that's cold!" as I nodded, he said, "Let's hurry." And we did.

Walking as fast as we dared in the blowing snow, we navigated both downhill slopes and managed to stay upright. Without a word, he took me straight to the dorm I lived in, gave my books back, opened the door, wished me a good evening, and walked away.

When I reached our room, my roommate was just hanging up her coat. She'd walked back with a group. Yet there was no trace of their having been anywhere on that path. I told her about my trek and described my escort, but she had no idea who he could have been, nor could any others I talked to.

I had never seen that man before and never saw him afterward. And I'd have remembered, because he was very nice looking. Where he came from, I don't know. How he knew which dorm I lived in, I have no clue. But that handsome guardian angel was good in more than just looks.

Our Miracle Journal

ED GAGE

A cold rain drizzled steadily in late December 1984 as my wife, Mike, and I sat at the dining table and contemplated the New Year. It promised to be as dismal as the weather outside. We were in the midst of the hol iday season, but there was nothing to celebrate and certainly nothing to look forward to.

Two years earlier, just before Christmas, Mike had been injured in an auto accident. The doctors said the daily pain she felt would last the rest of her life. We had no disability insurance, and so, between the loss of her income and the large medical bills, our finances were a wreck. Still worse, my university job was on the line due to Louisiana state-government budget cutbacks.

Staring down at the cold dregs in my coffee cup, I racked my brain to think of a way to improve our gloomy circumstances. But it was no use. Things were only getting worse.

Out of desperation, lately we had begun praying and meditating after hearing a seminar speaker say that, no matter what the situation, it was possible to change your life by first attuning to God and then watching for changes.

Maybe it gave Mike some hope, but my viewpoint was that it didn't work.

I picked up a handful of the bills littering the table and disgustedly let them drop. "I'm sick and tired of 'just getting by,'" I said to Mike. "We have to make something happen!"

From the midst of the bills, Mike picked up the checkbook register and idly thumbed the pages. "At least our money problem is simple," she said, "just a matter of not enough deposits to balance the withdrawals."

Suddenly she was excited and sitting up straight. "You know, that's the real problem we're having with life," she said, waving the checkbook in my direction. "We need more deposits of good events in our lives. The prayer and meditation are good, but we need more neat things happening in an active way."

"Great," I said caustically. "Why don't we start looking for miracles?"

Mike's blue eyes shone with enthusiasm. She had taken my sarcasm for sincerity. "That's perfect!" she said. "We say we believe God can work in our lives. Let's keep a record! We'll mark down anything that makes us feel joyous, that gives us a sense of the miraculous. Then in tough times we'll just take a look at the record." She looked directly at me. "Okay?"

Frankly, to me it sounded a bit crazy. But I already had said something must change, and I had no suggestions myself. "Okay. I'll try," I said doubtfully.

And that's how our Miracle Journal came to be—a section in a brown loose-leaf notebook in which we already kept lists of chores to do, errands to run, and bills to pay. It was just a few pages with a divider-tab marked "Miracles."

But if we thought we were going to find miracles, far from it! Late the Saturday night before New Year's Day we were returning home to Shreveport from a trip to Tyler, Texas. There was little traffic on the interstate and it was cozy in the heated car. Then I glanced at the temperature gauge! Disaster! It was entering the red danger zone! *Terrific,* I thought bitterly as images of being stranded at night flashed into mind.

Fortunately, within a mile we reached an exit ramp. I steered the car gingerly up it and toward a quick-stop grocery on the outskirts of Kilgore.

"What rotten luck!" I said to Mike. "We may be stuck here till Monday."

"Well, I think we are lucky," Mike said. "You've got only one relative in all of East Texas and he lives right here in Kilgore. So stop and go call."

One phone call later we learned that, luckily, my Uncle Ed had returned fifteen minutes earlier from a Christmas trip to Dallas, bringing two of my favorite aunts from Dallas with him. The five of us had a wonderful surprise holiday visit that night and the next day. Sunday afternoon, after refilling the radiator and tightening hoses, which we thought were leaking, we drove the sixty-five miles home.

At the repair shop Monday, the mechanic said the problem was not loose hoses but a blown head gasket on the motor. "You were lucky to make it back to town," he told us, "especially without damaging the engine."

Luck? Or our first miracle?

Back at the house, Mike did not share my uncertainty. "It was all a miracle," she said. "All of it. Write it down."

"It could be just coincidence," I said.

"How many coincidences in a row does it take for you to believe something positive is happening?" she said.

So I got out the Miracle Journal and wrote it down. Reluctantly.

It wasn't that I didn't believe in miracles; they always seemed to happen to somebody else. Still, for Mike's sake, I tried to keep an open mind about this prayer, meditation, and miracle business. But down deep I knew there was no free lunch.

I was able to make that point to Mike one Friday night when our spirits were as low as the balance in the checkbook.

"I sure wish we could go for pizza," Mike mused. "That would cheer us up."

"Great," I said, "but payday is nearly a week away, so no pizza tonight."

After I'd brought Mike down to earth, both our spirits sagged lower.

A few minutes later the phone rang. Friends Randy and Judy had just received good news. Would we like to help them celebrate by going out for pizza? Their treat!

Mike was exuberant. "Go write it down!" she said.

"What do you mean?" I asked. "It's just a coincidence."

"Ha!" Mike said, and went to get the Miracle Journal herself.

"Being asked out for pizza is not a miracle," I called after her. "Turning water into wine or something like that—that's a miracle. When something like that happens, then we'll know we're really on to something."

Meantime, we continued to pray and meditate regularly and to jot down the day-to-day happenings that left us feeling in a more positive frame of mind. Even I had to admit that those little notes on positive happenings in our lives were starting to have a cumulative effect. But miracles? I was still skeptical.

In February it snowed, something of a miracle in Louisiana. The heavy, blowing flakes laid a thick mantle of white over the entire city, closing streets, schools, and businesses. I used the day off from work to complete a magazine article, my first freelance writing effort in years.

As the snow continued to fall, Mike and I bundled up for a tramp through the novel weather to drop the finished article in a postal box a few blocks away. The heavy flakes swirled around us as we moved along the center of the snow-covered, deserted street.

Nearing the mailbox, we joked about what a momentous occasion it was, what with the falling snow, the unexpected holiday, and the article submission. "All that's missing is something to toast the story on its way," I kidded as I dropped the envelope inside the box.

Turning around, we began the snowy walk home. We had gone barely half a block when the door of a nearby house swung open, spilling out peals of laughter and a jubilant group of adults carrying a sled out into the wintry scene. "Come join our sledding party," they called, and then offered us sparkling cider from snow-chilled glasses.

We thanked them, but declined their party invitation and walked on. Then Mike turned to me, a mischievous gleam in her eye. "It's not exactly water into wine," she laughingly said, "but you have to admit that turning snow into cider is pretty close."

Coincidence again? *It had to be,* I thought, even though we knew none of the group, and offering drinks to strangers in a snowstorm is not exactly an old Southern tradition. But these coincidences were beginning to pile up. Although still doubtful, I was beginning to have doubts about my doubts.

The weeks passed, and our pray, meditate, watch-for-miracles routine continued; then a strange thing began to happen. As the pages of the Miracle Journal expanded, so did my gradual understanding of how God can work with us in everyday situations if only we make the effort to be receptive to Him. The seminar speaker had spoken of attunement as a two-step process: "To talk to God, pray," he had said. "To listen to God, meditate and pay attention to those inner promptings."

But at income tax time in April, that didn't make much sense as I found myself seated at the dining table facing piles of receipts and bank statements. Finally, after working on the tax sheets for hours, I put down my pencil, turned off the calculator and, with a sigh of relief, prepared to seal the paperwork. Suddenly I had an urge to check the figures one more time.

Ridiculous, I thought. I already had checked over the return three times.

The seminar speaker's words drifted through my mind: "Pay attention to inner promptings."

With a groan I picked up the pencil and calculator again. I reworked the tax figures one more time—and found an overlooked deduction that increased our refund by $250. The Miracle Journal was making a believer of me.

As the months progressed, meditating for guidance and then following inner promptings also began to produce an unexpected type of miracle in our journal. Just as miracles could come to us through others, so we could be helpful in miracles flowing to other individuals.

Sometimes it was something small, such as making a phone call or writing a letter to a friend who came strongly to mind. Later we would learn the particular call or letter had arrived at an opportune moment, that what had seemed insignificant to us had meant a great deal to the recipient—just like our pizza miracle in reverse.

Mike and I came to look forward to our sessions at the dining table, jotting down events from our daily lives. The Bible verse "Seek, and ye shall find" (Matthew 7:7) took on new meaning as we rediscovered life's everyday miracles so easily overlooked—a pleasant evening with friends, the first spring flowers blooming in the backyard, listening to relaxing music just before going to sleep.

And we increasingly discovered that our interpretation of events normally classified as "good" or "bad" was undergoing a major adjustment, such as that summer with no employment or income from the university. Previously I would have considered that "bad."

However (coincidentally?), that summer my parents were building their retirement home in a rural area about eighty miles away. They were doing much of the work themselves and needed assistance. So we packed our bags and spent the summer with them.

I was able to help my dad with painting and carpentry. And we all enjoyed the visiting, the garden vegetables, the slower-paced country life. Had I been employed at the university, we would have missed that enjoyable summer.

By autumn, even the Miracle Journal was turning into a miracle. Wonderful, providential events, large and small, were changing our attitudes for the better. But until the Miracle Journal, we had been largely unaware of their presence.

And then it was the holiday season again. One quiet evening Mike and I were relaxing in the living room, a fire radiating its cheery warmth while the stereo played softly. Mike was curled up on the sofa, reading a book under the glow of a nearby lamp. I was studying our Miracle Journal of the past year.

Looking back, I knew that our physical circumstances still had not changed appreciably from when we first began the Miracle Journal. But we were living and enjoying a whole new life.

Across the room, as she reached for a shawl, Mike winced as she felt a twinge of pain from her old auto-accident injury. Then she looked up, saw me and smiled. "What are you doing?" she asked.

I thought about all the blank pages lying ahead in the Miracle Journal waiting to be filled, perhaps even a special healing page for Mike.

"Just thinking about the New Year," I said, "and miracles."

There was much to look forward to.

A Love of a Lifetime

AUSTIN-NICHOLE ZACHRICH

I t was September 28, 2001. We had just driven twelve hours to Columbia, South Carolina, where my grandfather lay in a coma that had been sudden and unexpected. My grandfather had always been a tower of strength to me and, I believe, to everyone with whom he came in contact. He was a kind man and his faith could be felt by just being in the same room with him.

I stood at his bedside holding his hand, and I could feel him trying to hold mine back as I sang to him. The doctors and nurses all said he could not even know we were in the room, but somehow I knew that he was aware.

My parents and brother wept and my grandmother stood there not knowing what to do; this was the man she had been married to for more than fifty-five years. She was watching as he wilted away. I watched her touch him and talk to him, and it was just as we had always seen, a love that was so strong, so beautiful that we all wished for this type of relationship.

My grandfather had been in such pain for the past

few weeks, he had been diagnosed with severe arthritis. So you can see why we were all baffled at the comatose state in which he now lay. The night before it was announced that he had been battling acute leukemia for months but no one knew it until now.

My grandmother was in denial, because he was all she knew. However, she lovingly sat by his bedside and held his hand. She looked at him as if he were coherent and said, "Bob, I will let you go; it's okay. Just please, save a spot next to you for me in heaven." She leaned in and kissed him on the mouth for the last time as at that very moment my grandfather took his last breath. It was almost like my grandmother had given him permission to let go of her and hold onto our heavenly Father's hand.

It was the coming months that amazed our whole family. My grandmother, who we thought would fall apart without my grandfather, had somehow inherited his strength. She began reaching out and helping others who were grieving, becoming a leader in the church, doing community service and anything else she could find. My grandmother is eighty years old; she heads up a widows' and widowers' lunch group; she bakes a cake every week for the local fire fighters; she attends every funeral at her church hoping to share her strength. I am amazed.

I feel that my grandparents' efforts to be such pillars of strength for each other have inspired so many others to seek out what they can and should be doing. Because of their love, not only for one another, but for life and people, the love they shared will live on forever. They truly have a love of a lifetime.

She Gave the Softest Hugs

PAM GORESH

It's a cool morning in May, and as I clean up the kitchen, I'm looking forward to working in the garden and yard. Taking off my apron, I fondly remember my mother-in-law, Phyllis, who gave me this purple and green apron because it no longer fit her.

Ever since Phyllis passed away, the apron has taken on a special meaning and brings back memories. If one image comes to mind, it's of Phyllis waiting for us to arrive from out of town. Wearing a housecoat, slippers, and a long apron hanging from her shoulders to her knees, she would invite us into her warm kitchen. I never thought of her as being an "old fatty" as she often referred to herself with self-deprecating humor. Rather, she exemplified all the traits of the quintessential grandma. Phyllis was caring and giving, and she had an aura of peaceful serenity. My younger daughter summed it up well when she once said, "Grandma gives the softest hugs!" Even in her later years, I could still see the beauty in her strong Greek features of wavy black hair, the smoothest creamy skin, and big brown eyes.

Her kitchen always looked the same: dinner warming on the stove and cookies in tins cluttering the kitchen table. She was especially famous for her homemade koulourakia (butter twist cookies, which my kids called "twisty" cookies) and the best chocolate chip cookies I've ever eaten—I've never been able to duplicate them. Quite modest in her accomplishments, she'd say she couldn't cook gourmet meals. In wearing her apron today, I can only hope her talent rubs off on me.

I can still hear her voice, "Hi, Paaaam!" And we'd hug and kiss. We'd sit at the kitchen table, and we'd talk about the latest family news. She'd reach out and tap me on the arm to make a point, her affectionate way of emphasizing something. Her interests revolved around her family, and she was perfectly content in making them the focus of her life.

On the surface, one would think we didn't have a lot in common. I'm involved in a wide variety of activities and spend time away from home almost every day. Phyllis, on the other hand, preferred to stay close to home. But the warmth of home and family life was our common bond. In addition to that, we both loved to have a good laugh, and we both liked the color purple—we often would exchange purple items for gifts.

Even though, at times, we were separated by several states and neither one of us liked to pay for long distance telephone calls, we managed to keep in touch by writing letters to each other. She always addressed them just to me. "I went to town today to pay our electric and water bills and stopped by Stone and Thomas to pay on the lay-away" and "We had three inches of snow and it's been colder than usual" were typical lines from her letters. They came often enough that I began to expect them, and I could almost predict their arrival.

Early on in my marriage, Phyllis said I could call her Mom. Having married so young (at twenty-one) and having a loving and close relationship with my own mother, I couldn't imagine calling her "Mom" when she invited me to do so. But I was quick to tell my new mother-in-law that it didn't mean I loved her any less. She never mentioned it again, and I think I proved to her over the fifteen years I knew her how genuine my feelings were. We truly got along quite well and got to be good pen pals. I'd write newsy letters filled with details of all our activities. Phyllis would write back, telling me how much she loved reading my letters or how she laughed as she read about the antics of her grandchildren.

Christmas was her favorite holiday, and she loved to bake, decorate, and shop for presents for everyone she knew. And if we weren't going to be able to get together for the Easter holiday, we'd receive a special package through the mail. It would be filled with chocolate candy and several loaves of her special homemade Easter bread. It was so good, the kids and I wouldn't bother using a knife or butter; we'd just rip right into it. I'm sure Phyllis would have laughed if she had seen us.

Phyllis never finished high school but kept the family budget perfectly balanced and put three kids through college on a steelworker's paycheck. She instilled in her children tremendous values, as well as a deep respect for themselves and others.

It was May 1990 when Andy's mom and dad decided to visit. Mother's Day that year was the same weekend as our daughter Samantha's ninth birthday. Andy, Samantha, and her sister, Alexandra, went shopping and bought pretty lavender and green scented candles and soaps and baskets, a few things they knew Grandma would like.

As usual, Phyllis and Andrew were scheduled to arrive from West Virginia around lunchtime on Friday. Instead of a knock at the door announcing their arrival, the phone rang, and a voice said, "Mrs. Goresh? I'm calling from the Hagerstown Hospital in Maryland. Your father-in-law is fine, but your mother-in-law became ill on the trip and died of a heart attack."

Hours later, I sat alone in the living room. What could I say? What could I do?

Andy had driven to Hagerstown to meet his father. When Andy and his dad returned, words stuck in my throat and tears spilled from my eyes to see Andrew walk in alone. Andrew, with red-rimmed eyes, hugged me and said, "Phyllis was so happy that morning. She was looking forward to celebrating Samantha's birthday; and you know, she just loved all those letters you wrote. They meant so much to her."

When I talked with Phyllis's sister, Mary, about funeral arrangements, Mary mentioned that Phyllis had always loved the color pink. "Phyllis should be laid to rest in a pink dress," she added.

How about that? All those years she'd let me think her favorite color was purple so we would have something in common. As I passed her casket, I picked up a pink flower, paused, and thought, *No, Phyllis and I shared purple.* I put the pink flower down and reached instead for a lovely lavender iris and gave it to her.

Discovering the Real Miracles

NORRIS BURKES

I n an impatient tone that fell short of her namesake quality, Grace, a nurse in the intensive care unit, asked tersely, "Chaplain, what are you doing at 2 P.M.?"

"Uh . . ." Caught off guard, my afternoon schedule suddenly vanished from my memory. As chaplain for a Houston hospital in the early 1990s, my days stayed pretty full, but at that moment, I couldn't remember what I was doing in the next minute, let alone several hours later.

"We have an end-of-life conference with a family. Can you make it?" Frustrated by the lengthy use of an ICU bed, Grace had called the conference to discuss continuing life support for a seventy-five-year-old male stroke victim who had shown no sign of brain activity for sixty days.

"Life support" is a misnomer. At times like this, it should be called "mechanical maintenance." This man wasn't being supported; he was being preserved. Yet despite those efforts, his body was literally decaying.

Typically, most TV-watching Americans describe the process of discontinuing life support as "pulling the plug." They picture a nurse grimly yanking twenty tubes from every orifice or throwing a big switch somewhere that turns off all the electronic apparatuses, sending the patient's room into a quiet hush except for the flat-line hum of the monitor. Actually, it's far less dramatic, involving the slow turning of a few knobs. Done properly, it's usually a peaceful process.

When this family showed up in the conference room, it was quickly apparent that their hearts weren't anywhere near ready for our discussion. This family was "claiming a miracle." They didn't care what anyone said. They were claiming that their father would rise from his deathbed in three days. That was their definition of a miracle, defined and customized.

Shifting the conversation, I asked them what it might be like if they redefined what a miracle might be in this situation. What would a miracle look like, I asked, if they allowed the frame to be removed from their picture of God—if they accepted that the mysterious and unlimited workings of God might produce a miracle that differed from the one they had in mind?

Consider Jesus's example, and you'll see that even He was sometimes uncomfortable with the use of miracles. He didn't intend them as something that would prove the existence of God. He told one group of scoffers that even if he were to raise someone from the dead, they still wouldn't believe. The fact is, we may learn as much from studying Jesus's avoidance of miracles on certain occasions as we do by reading how and when he did perform them. For instance, at Calvary he was taunted by people who demanded that he come down from the cross. "He saved others," they sneered, "but he can't save himself!" (Matthew 27:42). It never occurred to them that a miracle was occurring. Even His closest followers couldn't see (although Jesus had told them it would happen).

Like those disciples, we, too, often overlook the real miracles. Maybe, while we're waiting and watching for one preconceived miracle to happen, something else happens, but we fail to see the miraculous in it.

For instance, maybe the true miracle isn't always going to be that Dad survives cancer but that his prodigal children come back into his life. Perhaps the real miracle will not be a baby's survival after a difficult birth but that somehow she will introduce a presence of God to her family or even to hospital staffers.

Miracles aren't always about getting something back; sometimes they are about finding a fuller appreciation for what you have left when that something is taken away. Maybe the true miracle isn't always going to be about saving the world but about gaining new appreciation for a piece of it.

During the week following the end-of-life conference

(in which the family did finally agree to discontinue life support), I saw at least two small miracles. That father didn't walk out of our hospital, no, but three sisters found agreement in prayer as they united at their father's bedside and gave him permission to walk into the arms of a waiting God. That was the first small miracle. And the second and more lasting miracle was that the sisters discovered an infinite God whom they could not control.

And in my experience, knowing a God whom you cannot control is the first step toward knowing that God is miraculously in control.

CHAPTER 5

Day by Day with God

The LORD is great; he should be praised . . . on his holy mountain. . . . This God is our God forever and ever. He will guide us from now on (Psalm 48:1, 14 NCV).

As human beings we often relegate God to special segments of our lives. We tend to acknowledge His presence on Sunday, Easter, and Christmas. We notice He's there at weddings and funerals or when someone's seriously ill. How often we forget, though, that God is omnipresent—always present. He is with us every minute of every day. And what a joy it is to be aware of His constant companionship and walk joyfully day by day with God.

Getting Out of God's Way

BARBARA CURTIS

C hristine's shriek whipped into the room, slicing my phone call midsentence. "BARBARA! Hurry! Your car's rolling down the hill!"

Throwing down the receiver, I spun and raced down the hall. As if something had picked me up, shook, and booted me into a more focused dimension, I could see only the door at the end of the hall, hear only the pulse surging in my ears.

Seconds slowed and separated, like drops from a leaky faucet. Grabbing the only emergency cord I could, I begged, "Oh God, dear God, please let it be empty."

Moments ago I had been leaving Christine's office, my toddler in my arms, my oldest son by my side. At the door we had taken extra time for Jonathan to wave bye-bye. When the phone rang, Christine had turned back inside. The parking lot gravel was crunching under my feet when she appeared again at the door to say my husband was on the phone.

"Honey, will you put him in his car seat? I'll be right back." I turned to Joshua, eleven, everyone's right-hand man. Christine had asked him to come to physical therapy today to distract Jonathan from the discomfort and tedium of his workout.

"Sure, Mom," Joshua said. I put his brother into his arms. At three, Jonathan was still too wobbly to negotiate the rocky parking lot safely. Down's syndrome meant his physical as well as his mental development was delayed. But for his family, his cute little face spelled courage and perseverance. We regarded his features as some would a badge of honor: he had to work so hard for things that came so easily to others. Knowing the importance of early intervention for DS children, we had brought Jonathan here weekly since his earliest, floppiest days. You might say we were trying to smooth the road a bit for Jonathan to become all God meant him to be.

Why had my husband called that day? Neither of us remember. He only recalls my cry of dismay and the phone clattering on the floor. Then my screams.

"No! Oh, no! Oh, God, please, no!"

The car wasn't empty. Through the windshield, I could see the top of Jonathan's blond head, framed by his car seat. He was being carried backward down the sloping driveway toward the two-lane road below. On the other side of the road was a thirty-foot drop to the San Francisco Bay.

As though I were falling down it myself, I felt the agony of what would happen to my little boy in the minute ahead. If the car cleared the roadway without being struck, it would crash down the embankment and end in the Bay.

"Oh Lord, not here, not now," I pleaded. Moments from Jonathan's brief but difficult life flashed through the memory of my senses. I could hear the beeps of the monitors in Intensive Care, see the tangle of cords and wires from the limp body, feel the tug on my stomach when the doctors prepared us for the worst. So many times we had been through these things, with so many people praying for our special little boy. And, one by one, God had healed him of his frailties. For the past year he had been so healthy we had actually begun to relax.

Could God really choose to take him now, after all He'd seen us through?

Not if my son Joshua could help it. Horrified, I saw him behind the car, straining his ninety-five pounds against the ton of metal grinding him backward. Running awkwardly in reverse as the car picked up speed, he was on the verge of being crushed any second.

I couldn't lose two sons! "Joshua, let go! Get away from the car!" I screamed. Christine was screaming too. Even as we pleaded with him, I understood my son's heart. He always took responsibility. Everything within him would rage against giving up the battle to save his brother.

I screamed again, "Joshua! Obey me! Let go!"

At last, he jumped away from the car. As Joshua let go, Christine and I stopped screaming. The quiet was eerie. The moment hung poised like the last drop of water from the faucet. The car seemed to hesitate, the rear wheels to shift. Now the car was moving at an angle toward the edge of the driveway, losing momentum, grinding to a halt. Almost gracefully, it came to rest against an old and faithful-looking tree.

Bolting for the car, flinging open the door, I found Jonathan unhurt but bewildered—he had never been in a moving car all by himself before! Catching sight of Joshua right behind me, he grinned and stretched his arms wide— his way of saying, "Life—what an adventure!"

I've been behind a rolling car before. I've tried to pit my puny weight against circumstances that were way too big for me to handle. Perhaps that's why I understood Joshua's reaction all too well.

"Mom, all I could think of was that I couldn't let him die," Joshua told me later.

"All I could think of . . ." That's me all over, willing to sacrifice everything for some good purpose. And ever over-estimating my indispensability. Even if I know I need God's help, don't I often think He needs mine as well? Don't I often act as though God can accomplish the supernatural only if I stay involved?

Maybe sometimes He is just waiting for me to get out of the way and let Him take care of things before I get myself hurt. Maybe He'd like to do something truly miraculous, something I'd always remember, something I couldn't take credit for myself. Maybe He'd like me to be more like Jonathan, just going along for the ride, a little worried perhaps, but remembering I'm in good hands and ready for the rescue.

I hadn't put my car in park; that little bit of carelessness almost cost me two sons. But God chose instead to teach me a lesson about His mercy and His might. He gave me a picture I will never forget—one son trying to avert disaster, letting go in desperation, and being saved. The second, powerless and utterly dependent on God's own outcome.

Because Jonathan is who he is, he might always keep that sweet simplicity. And I will ever be learning from his triumphant trust as he stretches out his arms and smiles, "Life—what an adventure!"

Promises to Keep

TERI KURTZ

Teri?"

"Huh?" I sat up in bed and pressed the phone tighter to my ear as I glanced at the clock. *5:30.*

"Sorry to call so early. There's been an accident. . . . Your stallion got out of the pasture this morning. He was hit by a truck."

"What?" Instantly I was awake. "Is he okay?"

"I don't know."

With shaking fingers I hung up and quickly dialed my veterinarian. We agreed to meet at the farmer's field where Star was boarded.

"Lord, please let him be all right," I pleaded on the twenty-minute drive. I gripped the steering wheel and looked out at the bleak January day. I couldn't handle another loss in my life. There had been so many in the last two years: a daughter that had run away from home, my farm, and the liquidation of many of my prized Appaloosa horses. Most days I just survived and tried not to focus on all the things that had changed or disappeared in my life.

I pulled into the driveway. Someone had tied Star to a log in the front yard. As I approached, the big stallion nickered to me.

"I'm here, buddy, don't worry." I stroked his nose and looked him over carefully. There was a bloody gash in his shoulder that would require stitches and numerous cuts and scrapes on his face and body. The horse was obviously in pain but I felt hopeful. Dr. Kelly, after a careful exam, was more cautious.

"Teri, we won't know anything for a few days yet. He could have internal injuries. If he makes it through the next four days, we should be out of the woods." I called a friend and arranged to move Star to her barn where he could recuperate.

"Ever's Stardust" was a dream come true from the moment he was born. I had owned his father and mother and watched as he entered the world seventeen years before. Star had seemed like a gift from God right from the beginning. He had a perfectly formed black body, sprinkled with spots, and a kind, gentle disposition. I could easily ride him around mares and trusted him with children. He was exactly the kind of herd sire I always wanted. More than that, he was my friend.

On the third day after the accident I drove to the barn to meet with Dr. Kelly and check on Star's progress. I put on his halter, taking note of the untouched hay in the manger.

"Walk him out a little; let's have a good look."

I took the lead and Star moved out haltingly. With each step I heard a strange sloshing noise that seemed to come from his stomach. Then Star stopped and with a groan bent his knees to lie down. I pulled hard on the lead, fighting panic.

"What's happening, Dr. Kelly?" She quietly examined the horse for a few minutes before speaking.

"He's bleeding internally, Teri. . . . It may be time to say good-bye."

I couldn't look at her. "Yeah. . . ." Tears burned behind my eyes. "I don't want him to suffer." I stroked Star's muscular neck and stared into a nearby pasture where mares were grazing peacefully. I heard Dr. Kelly go to her truck for the syringe full of barbiturates. A moment later, Star was gone.

On the drive home the grief was overwhelming. Another loss. The road took me by my old farm by the river. I looked out at the overgrown fields. Star used to run in them, as did his many foals. The thought of his babies made me cry even harder. Ironically I had given away the mare that was pregnant with his last foal. Star had sired more than thirty foals, and I no longer owned even one.

I always loved Appaloosa horses. It had been my passion since college to breed them. The horses were like family, and I had owned generations of the same bloodlines. Then a daughter ran away from home and the resulting family crisis began draining us emotionally and financially. That was followed by a change in my husband Steve's job. Fewer hours meant less money and we fell farther behind. The bank repossessed the farm. Piece by piece, the life I had known fell down like a line of dominos.

"Lord, I don't even know who I am anymore," I cried, pounding the steering wheel of my truck. Everything that defined who I was had changed. The few remaining pieces I was trying to hold on to didn't add up to much of a future. I even questioned my involvement with horses. Maybe it was time to hang that up too.

After Star's death, it became harder and harder to get up in the morning. Some days I just stayed in bed, looking out the window of our small rented cabin tucked in a stand of evergreens. My life felt as cold and dark as the landscape outside. I functioned on autopilot: get the kids to school, drive to the rented pasture and feed my remaining horses, make dinner, fall into bed. Church on Sunday was the only thing I looked forward to.

One cold January night I made the half-hour drive to feed and check on the horses. I noticed my old broodmare, Lady, was looking thin. Her round black belly hung down, skin stretched tight over knobby ribs. "You're looking a little bony, old girl." I stroked her thick winter coat. Time to add higher calorie alfalfa to her normal ration.

Lady was one of the few older horses I kept. She was lame and couldn't be bred anymore, but she had been with me her entire life and produced several fine foals. She deserved to be cared for in retirement.

In February I took note of Lady's condition again. As I methodically threw out piles of hay I stared at her bulging belly. She was fatter now, just not in the right places. I walked over and ran my hand down her slightly swayed back, pressing it against her belly. It moved, ever so slightly, under my hand.

"No, it can't be!" Lady regarded me seriously, stalks of hay hanging out of the corners of her mouth.

"How could you be pregnant?" I put my hands on my hips and looked hard at her. Her wise old eyes looked into mine, dark with a secret. I thought back to my early boarding arrangements. I had been careful to keep Star away from the mares. With my situation I couldn't afford any unexpected surprises. The mares had been in their field and Star in his, five strands of hot wire encouraging him to keep his distance. Then, at the farmer's insistence, I moved the mares to another property altogether. Nevertheless, Lady stood before me, her swollen belly a promise.

Immediately I increased Lady's feed and began worrying about the birth. Once again one of my horses needed special care, and I had no facilities to provide it.

Lady was enormous by the time I finally found a place

for her to foal. It was a small paddock and shelter only five minutes from my house. I checked on her often, fearful she would lose the baby.

On a beautiful day in May I made my routine stop at Lady's paddock on my way to town. Her milk had come in and she seemed preoccupied and uncomfortable. When night fell I called a friend, who agreed to spend the night in the car with me and keep watch.

I slept fitfully, panning the flashlight around the field each time I awoke to check on Lady's position. During the wee hours of the morning my flashlight found her stretched out on the grass in the middle of birthing. Carefully I opened the car door and walked to the paddock, talking softly so as not to startle her. As I knelt down the baby slipped out, its muzzle breaking open the placenta. Immediately the foal let out a nicker as if announcing its arrival. Rocking back on my heels I laughed out loud, "Well aren't you something?"

The night air was chilly, so I wiped the baby down with an old towel. I rubbed briskly, checking the foal over as I worked. Lady had produced a filly, coal-black with three white socks and a wide blaze. Perfect in every way.

It didn't take long for the filly to rise on wobbly legs and begin nursing, her stubby tail enthusiastically flicking from side to side. I sat back and watched, drinking in the night air and the magic of the birth. It reminded me of another night seventeen years before when I watched Star being born. I had been given a gift then, and God was blessing me now, bringing comfort in the midst of loss, a promise of brighter tomorrows.

My life had changed but God was with me and my future, whatever it held, was secure in His hands.

If You're Willing to Ask

ANDREA PETERSON

L ast year, my family enjoyed a dream vacation to
Hawaii. One afternoon, we visited the famous
Black Sand Beach, where black volcanic rocks tossed by
the churning waves digress to smooth "river" rocks and
finely ground black sand. Having seen nothing like
those waves before, my daughters were enamored with
holding hands with their daddy and trying to withstand
the force of the water.

A huge wave rolled in and easily toppled the girls,
completely covering both of them. After their daddy
helped them back to their feet, we realized a catastrophe:
our eldest was missing her glasses! Her vision was so bad
without them that she had left them on as she played in
the waves.

We all began frantically searching for those glasses.
Other vacationers enjoying the water learned of our
dilemma and some began to search as well, but we all
knew we were never going to see them again. Her thick,
heavy glasses would sink right to the bottom and, even

if we could find them in the waves and sand, the rocks would ruin them.

Our daughter was frantic, thinking that the rest of her vacation would be ruined. Trying to comfort her, I heard myself saying that the God of the universe, who created that massive ocean, knew exactly where those glasses were at that precise moment. And, if He chose to do so, He was the only one who could return them to us.

About forty-five minutes later, not really believing we would see the glasses again, my husband and I walked down the beach and talked about how we would replace her glasses. Suddenly, a huge wave rolled in, completely drenching our towels. As the water receded, on the sand at my husband's feet appeared Megan's glasses. They had a few scratches around the edges of the lenses and the frames had taken a beating, but she's been wearing them ever since!

Only God can explain how they made their way back to us. But that day, He taught me that everyday miracles do occur—if we're willing to ask for them.

Who Wove the Robe?

DOROTHEA M. HULSE

W e want an absolutely seamless robe, as exact as you can make it in texture, color, and weave to the one Christ wore."

This was my assignment from Charles Le Maire, wardrobe director at Twentieth Century Fox, some six months before this studio was to begin filming *The Robe*, based on the famous novel by the late Lloyd C. Douglas.

Weaving this robe was to be the biggest adventure of my life . . . an adventure climaxed by near calamity.

First came four months of intensive research as Mr. Le Maire and I combed every yarn house in this country and Europe before we found the exact grade of sheep's wool yarn. Then, more weeks of making samples for texture and color. We spent days brewing dyes of walnut hulls, such as were used in Galilee two thousand years ago.

So immersed did my family and I become in the life and times of Jesus and in the miracles of His power that we were only mildly surprised when "coincidences" nudged our work along.

First, our research was suddenly simplified when at home I came across a rare book *The Dictionary of the Bible* by James Hastings, published in 1909. Left to me by my father, Willard Aldrich, it contained descriptions of how yarn was spun, dyed, and woven in Galilee in the first century.

Next, Eddie Azzam, a young pupil in my Sunday school class at the Los Angeles First Methodist Church, happened to mention that he had lived in Palestine. The lad proved it by bringing me a seamless robe from Bethlehem, where it was sold as a copy of the robe actually worn by Christ.

Because the walnut dye photographed a lifeless brown, we decided to add henna to it. Later, by chance, we discovered that in a French monastery was a fragment believed to be from the robe itself, and that it had the selfsame reddish color.

When my daughter, Dorothy Lou Macready, and I finally started to weave the robe itself, our thoughts and words focused on the Man who wore the original. We discussed the woman whose Son Jesus healed. It was this mother's gratitude, according to one tradition, that prompted her to weave the robe. An arduous task, this style of weaving was originally done in certain sections of Egypt—and during the Master's lifetime only in the province of Galilee.

We recalled the scene at the foot of the cross, where

soldiers cast lots for the robe—how its symbolism had lived nearly two thousand years.

These quiet weekends of work on the loom contained many golden moments as we relived the story of Jesus.

At 4:30 one Sunday—the day before production was to begin on *The Robe*—Dorothy Lou and I wove the final thread. My small grandson drew close, small hands reaching out to touch.

It was finished. Next morning at nine it would be at the studio. We counted up the months of research and the hours of actual weaving . . . three hours for each five inches . . . thirty-six hours in all, not counting warping the loom.

At that moment a look of anguish froze my daughter's face. I turned hastily to see my three-year-old grandson standing with a pair of shears in one hand and a large piece of the robe in the other. All our effort gone in the twinkling of a bright pair of scissors!

Thousands of dollars in talent, sets and stars, the maximum effort of a large studio scheduled to begin work at nine in the morning, exactly sixteen hours away . . . and the robe, a thirty-six-hour job—not counting the time to rewarp the loom—gouged beyond repair.

Oddly enough, the thought that thirty-six hours of weaving couldn't be done in sixteen hours didn't occur to me until much later. The first thought that came was, *pray.* The second was *work.*

As Dorothy Lou and I started a new robe, our fingers flying, I thought back to a certain childhood experience when I was eight . . . a picnic with my best girlfriend, Mary Oliver. Before leaving, I had talked my cross and disagreeable landlady into lending me a luggage strap for my bicycle.

When we were ready to start for home late that afternoon, we couldn't find the luggage strap. Up and down the banks of the stream, in and out of the apple orchard we searched, to no avail. At last, in tears, we did the only thing we knew. We knelt down and prayed, then arose and walked back into the orchard. Sure enough, there it lay in the grass. To my young mind, it seemed completely understandable.

Now here I was, a grown woman and a grandmother, sitting before my loom praying . . . and expecting results. For it is my definite belief that "except ye remain as little children," or develop and renew that simple faith of a child, you miss the results that can happen through pure trust.

So my daughter and I prayed and worked through the night while her two children slept nearby, under some hand-woven shawls.

At exactly two o'clock in the morning Dorothy Lou and I were once more weaving the final threads on the robe. In just nine hours we had rewarped and completed a job that had taken thirty-six hours before. Later, when we did two extra robes, it took thirty-six hours again, although there was no variation in technique or honest application and effort.

When Dorothy looked at the hands of the clock as we completed that second robe, she said in a very small voice, "Nine hours, Mother . . . it isn't humanly possible."

I certainly agree.

Bloom Where Planted

PEGGY FREZON

O h, how I hated our backyard. No, that's too weak a word. I loathed that yard. When my husband, Mike, and I first saw this house one winter years earlier, we were charmed. There was antique wallpaper in every room, natural wood molding, even an old-fashioned pantry just off the kitchen. But the yard was . . . so small. No room for a swing set or monkey bars for our kids, Kate and Andy, when they got older. No room for our Lab, Hudson, to play. *Can't have everything,* I thought, staring at the snow-covered ground.

Anyway, we loved the house. We'd live in there, not the yard, right? So we decided to go ahead and buy it.

The first warm day after we'd moved in, the kids wanted to go out to play. Winters in Upstate New York bring along lots of cabin fever. I wanted to get out and get some fresh air too. We put on jackets and headed out back. What the . . . ? The snow had melted, leaving one lonely little patch of muddy ground smack in the middle of a sea of asphalt. *Who in their right minds would pave over their yard?*

"Let's go to the park instead," I told Kate and Andy.

Mike thought the yard got too much shade for grass to grow. Granted, it was lined with tall trees, and the garage blocked out the sunlight too. "Well, I don't care. We'll try it anyway," I announced. I seeded that pathetic patch of earth. The grass never really took, no more than a few scraggly tufts. It looked like the head of a middle-aged man who didn't even have enough hair for a comb-over.

I tried praying about it but gave up after a while. *What's the point?* I thought. God had bigger fish to fry. Besides, what did I expect? He wasn't going to change the earth's orbit just so my crummy yard could get more sunlight. If He didn't care, I wouldn't either, I decided.

I began avoiding the backyard as much as possible. The only time I'd set foot in it was to hang laundry out to dry. The kids played in the park. Our Lab got his exercise on long walks. And in the summer, we picnicked at the kitchen table.

It took me about a minute to rake the leaves that first fall. Kate and Andy took turns jumping into the pile. More of a bump than a pile, really. The kids didn't know what they were missing. A real backyard had swings, a fort, maybe even a swimming pool. Instead, ours was like a dirty parking lot with a clothesline.

It wasn't even much good for that. I couldn't begin to tell you how many times I had to wash something all over again because it had blown off the line and landed in the dirt. But seeing a white towel crumpled in the far corner of the yard one spring day was the last straw. *Figures!* I thought, seething while I tromped along the asphalt. *I am sick and tired of this. I can't even have nice laundry thanks to this poor excuse for a yard!*

I reached down to get the towel. Something underneath it caught my eye. A tiny purple flower poked up through a crack in the pavement. I bent down for a closer look. It had a bell-shaped blossom, petals that ruffled like a fancy skirt and a faint hint of lovely fragrance.

You sure picked the wrong place to bloom, I thought. *Won't be long till you're dead and gone.*

I turned around and stomped back to the house. But before I went inside, something stopped me. The loathing I felt for our yard faded, just a little bit. The flower had managed to grow without room and without sunlight. A tiny bit of beauty had sprung up from such ugliness. What else might be able to grow here?

We could rip up the pavement and I could ask at the greenhouse what grows in shade, I thought.

The next day we threw on some old clothes and went to work. Mike swung away with a pickax and I carted off the chunks he dug up. Each heavy load I got rid of made me feel lighter. "Why didn't we do this before?" I asked.

"We're doing it now," Mike said. "That's what really matters."

The kids were excited to help. Kate turned the newly uncovered soil and Andy scattered grass seed. Every day after that I'd go out to check, kneeling to bask in the scent of dirt, feeling as if something had been planted in me too. Finally one day it happened: grass started growing.

Later that week we came across a construction worker throwing away old bricks. He let us take them, and we made walkways along the shadiest parts of our yard. I filled terra-cotta pots with hosta, ferns, and impatiens— all of them hardy enough to thrive even without much sun.

Lord, I marveled, *You've seen even to the needs of these plants.*

These days I spend as much time as I can in our yard. I'll sit in my big white wicker chair with a glass of soda and read or just daydream. It's moments like those that remind me of a lesson from the Bible: "He will satisfy your needs in a sun-scorched land," it says in Isaiah. "You will be like a well-watered garden."

Well, our yard still isn't exactly sun-scorched. But I'd say we've had our share of growth.

Out of the Mouths of Babes

PAM FRANTZ

My husband and I were devastated and depressed when after four years of marriage we remained childless. We both wanted a big, bustling family. After endless rounds of tests and procedures, the doctors reported we were sterile and would never be able to bear children.

A great thing came of that news: Michael and I were able to adopt a precious and precocious baby boy we named Jordan. Jordan was the perfect son, and, best of all, as soon as he could talk he seemed to think he was a preacher. He strutted around quoting scriptures, offered up loud and boisterous prayers, and generally took on the character of a "preacher boy."

When Jordan was four he started carrying around a rolled-up towel. We would ask him what it was, and he would roll his eyes and say, "You know." Finally after weeks of this behavior, we wondered if this was a little sick. He would not give up the towel, nor would he give us further explanation.

One night I was near tears over Jordan's strange behavior, so I sat him down and told him that sometimes God speaks through little children to us obtuse adults.

Again, he said, "You know, Mom."

"No, Jordan, I don't know. Perhaps you have a message for me."

Very seriously Jordan placed the rolled-up towel in my arms and said, "This is my baby sister. She's coming soon."

I was struck. We had diligently taught Jordan that he was so special to us because he was the only child we could have. I explained again.

"No, Mom, you don't understand," he said with those gorgeous brown eyes pleading. "God told me I would get a baby sister, and she's coming soon." He solemnly rerolled the towel, put it in his arms, and strolled away.

I shared Jordan's story with friends and church members, all of whom had prayed for Michael and me for years. "They shook their heads in doubt, but in faith admonished us to let God be in control.

Imagine how we felt when two months later I was found pregnant and well into the first trimester. Rejoicing time in our church and family!

The pregnancy went well, a first for me. Our miracle child came two months early but was healthy and normal.

We decided we wanted to name her Moriah, but what was the second name to be? We turned to our little preacher boy, who had confidently prophesied for weeks before anybody would take him seriously.

"Hope," he responded with a gleam in his eyes. "She's the Hope of God in us to never give up on the gifts He has for us."

So Moriah Hope it is, and we will never again doubt that "out of the mouths of babes . . . come miracles!"

The Miracle of the Sofa

ZARETTE BEARD

I had been shopping for the perfect sofa for months. I couldn't just settle on any old run-of-the-mill sofa; it had to be just right. The right color, the right fabric, style, and very high on the comfy scale. I found my dream sofa, measured it, bought it, and could hardly wait for Saturday's delivery. I imagined all of the family fun and memories we would create on that sofa. My family would be forever bonded on that piece of furniture.

Saturday came and the memory-making sofa arrived. I was pleased to see two very clean, well-groomed young movers ready to bring my sofa into its new home. I was grateful, as I had imagined a big sweaty brute wearing a flannel shirt with the sleeves torn off and jeans that rode much too low, talking to me through clenched, brown teeth that held a cigar stub.

Cheerily, I led the sofa movers to the basement. They thought it best to use the sliding glass door. After much wrangling, handle removing, and prying, we realized the glass door was not going to come apart. Having no worries, I suggested we just bring the sofa through the house. There should be no problem, as the house has very high ceilings and an extra-wide staircase.

The movers got my sofa to the bottom of the stairs and that's when the trouble started. It would not fit through the door at the bottom of the stairs. They wrangled that sofa, tipped it this way and that, but it simply wouldn't fit. I was horrified. I had measured incorrectly. We squeezed the pillowy sofa and pushed as hard as we could, but it would not budge because the sofa frame was 33" x 37" and the doorway was 29" wide. I asked the guys to wait for just a second as I ran up the stairs. I dropped to my knees and uttered a quick, yet heartfelt prayer, the same kind of prayer I prayed as a small child. *Dear God, I'm stuck! Please help. You created the whole earth and parted the Red Sea. Please make my doorway bigger just long enough to get the sofa through.* And with that, I rose to my feet, went back downstairs and asked the guys to try again. They informed me that if they tried, my beautiful sofa would be torn up and have paint streaks on it. I assured them I would take responsibility, so they proceeded.

Now what do you think happened? It fit! It went straight through without a single tear or mark of paint on it! The movers were duly surprised and kept looking at the sofa, then each other, then the sofa . . .

I was so happy, I just started laughing and thanking God right there. I told them I had prayed and they added me to their visual exercise of looking at each other, then the sofa, then me, and so on. Just goes to show that the God of miracles who created the whole earth and parted the Red Sea also cares about the affairs of silly women who have no ability to measure whatsoever. And now you know the miracle of the sofa.

Relaxing in His Love

HOLLY BAXLEY

I sat alone on the floor of my dream home devastated, while my babies, ages two and three, were upstairs sleeping. I looked around at the beautiful late eighteenth century home that my husband and I had worked hard to restore with tears in my eyes. It still had many projects untouched, but to see just how far it had come in a year and a half made me extremely proud.

We had lived in a few homes that needed repair and restoration, but this one had a very special place in my heart. For years I had dreamed of living in a two-story, clapboard style home, with gingerbread work on the porch and a white picket fence in the back—the kind of home that my dreams revolved around as a young lady. The kind of dream that visualized a handsome prince for a husband, two kids, and a beautiful home with a white picket fence for the family dog; the kind of home where an American flag could wave proudly in the gentle breeze from its post on a porch column.

I dreamt of it often while growing up in a transitory mobile home. I dreamt of it from my tiny bedroom that was really supposed to be an office or sitting room. I dreamt of it when strong winds and storms threatened and rattled the mobile home's paper-thin walls. As I shook along with the winds that blew, I promised myself that one day I would live in a beautiful, old, established home with a lot of history—one that had weathered many storms and embraced generations of families. Many years and wedding anniversaries later, I felt that I finally achieved that dream the day we signed the agreement to purchase this house.

We made many renovations and added fixtures and touches here and there. Brent even went so far as to buy me an intricate, hanging tiffany lamp for our dining room. I saw one I wanted a few years ago at a furniture showroom, but the price tag was a bit too pricy for our budget at the time. And when he found a slightly smaller version for a fraction of the price, he bought it for me and hung it proudly in our formal dining room. It was a special love gift from him to me. I can't explain why it moved me so much, other than to say it just spilled light of inviting rest and relaxation. And he bought it just for me! Oh how I loved that lamp and all the nuisances of that we poured our lives into. It was my beautiful, established "forever" home.

And now I sat on the floor as sunlight streaked through the stained-glass window of the parlor. The colors danced across my legs as if to cheer me up. But there was no reviving from the gloom that had settled over my soul—for we needed to sell our home and fast.

For within the space of two weeks, we received two very deep personal blows to our lives. First we heard that Brent's mom had a relapse of melanoma cancer, after eighteen years in remission. Not only was it back, but it was at stage four—one of the worst kinds of relapses that can occur.

We were broken hearted with that announcement, for we were living several states away from his mom at the time and there was no way to be able to help her during this very uncertain time in her life. My mind flashed back to my mother's funeral, for I had lost my own mother to a horrendous battle with colon cancer. It was like a bad flashback revisited, for we were living a couple of states away from my mom as well, while Brent was earning his master's degree. I just could not imagine Brent going through this again with his own precious mother, all these years later, in the same manner. While we contemplated what to do, we received the word about him losing his job.

And honestly, that should have been a relief just for the fact that it would have given us clearer direction on what to do. But it was not a good parting. It was messy, emotional, highly charged, hurt many people profoundly, and broke our spirits as well as our hearts.

And that's why I was sitting on the floor of my parlor on the verge of tears. The weight of the world was crushing our souls, and the future was so very uncertain.

We knew that it wasn't just enough to try to figure out how to pick up the pieces, or how to support Brent's mother from afar. We began to toy with the idea that we needed to move back to our hometown quickly—to be close to his mom and figure out how to take care of our family from there.

But how were we going to do that? We couldn't afford to move at this point, and yet if we stayed, we wouldn't be able to make another mortgage payment. I was a stay-at-home mom, and even if I had found work, we couldn't have afforded to pay for daycare for our children. It was a bad catch twenty-two. No matter which way we thought about possible scenarios, they all turned out badly. We went to bed that evening heavy hearted.

The next morning, we started to discuss the need to move back to our hometown. It really made the most sense. Brent said that we needed to list the house with a local realtor, as it might take some time to sell. Besides, we wouldn't be able to oversee showing it to potential buyers, as we had previous homes we had owned. We tried to think through any possible connections that might know of someone who would be interested in our home. But we couldn't come up with a single one. We needed a miracle. We needed God to drop a buyer in our laps.

And at that thought, we tried to smile at each other, but ended up sighing. Mysterious buyers don't just pop in the door looking for a home to purchase. Brent pushed the hair back from my eyes and announced, "I've got to call the realtor today, so we can get this listed as soon as possible."

As soon as he spoke those words, our phone rang. Brent answered the phone and at first his face seemed quite bewildered. As the conversation progressed, his face widened into a bright smile. That startled me, for I hadn't seen him smile like that in quite a while. What in the world could have made his countenance shine like that?

After he hung up the phone, he relayed the conversation to me. A stranger had called asking Brent if we were going to put our house on the market. It seems that the nice lady had received the information from one of her co-workers that we would be moving soon. The co-worker, who knew Brent and me, had told her of the remodeling we had already done to the house. She then told Brent that this was an answer to her prayers, because she had been looking for an old home for over a year. For her, the hunt had not been successful. With her single status, most of the homes she had seen were either too much work for her, or did not have the charm that she wanted. She had heard so many good things about our house—could she come see it today?

I looked at Brent incredulously. *Oh, this can't be real—he's got to be teasing. But he's grinning like a Cheshire cat.*

"She's coming over today at one to look at the house," he beamed, "and she's bringing a friend."

"What . . . now?" I ask in disbelief.

"Yes, now! Well, at one. But yes, she's coming today!"

"But I haven't cleaned the house yet!" I panicked.

"Don't worry about it," he smiled. "We'll get it straightened up. Besides, if it's meant to be, it's meant to be."

All the intense emotions of the past few days just hit me again in a fresh wave and I started to cry. "I don't care if she isn't interested in buying our home after she sees it; it's just enough that she called. God is looking out for us! No matter what happens—God is looking out for us!"

We spent the rest of the morning straightening up and entertaining our children. At one o'clock, as promised, she came to the door with her friend. She leaned toward me, her kindly eyes twinkling and fairly whispered, "She won't be wearing the 'rose-colored glasses' that I will." And then she proceeded to go through each room, oohing and ahhing over the house and its character, or over an improvement we had done. She especially liked the last unfinished project. Brent was in the process of opening up the dark and dimunitive staircase into a much larger, brighter one.

Her friend was very quiet through the whole walk-through, sweeping the scene before her with her eyes. I wondered what she was thinking as she walked along with us, but she refrained from comments. Her eyes seemed to sparkle though, so I took that as a complement.

After the walk-through was over and all pertinent questions had been answered, she asked her friend what she thought. I held my breath.

"It's a very lovely home," the friend nodded thoughtfully to me.

"Well then," said the glowing potential buyer, "I will get back with you soon."

And with that perky announcement, the two friends walked out our door and into the gentle May sunshine.

After she left, Brent asked me what I was thinking.

"I'm thinking that God sent us a wonderful gift in sending that sweet woman here."

"That's true, but do you think she liked the house?"

I looked stunned at Brent for a moment. That's when I realized he was teasing. We both burst out laughing.

But even in that laughter and the wonderful afternoon that we shared with her, we couldn't believe it when she was ringing the doorbell again within twenty-four hours with a contract to buy the home and a good-faith deposit.

I held the contract in my trembling hands, dazed by what I just witnessed. The power of a loving God, One who knew our needs even before we did; a God who sent another woman an answer to her prayers in the form of this home; and did it so neatly and completely that no one can doubt who the author of this event was.

And as I write this story of God's grace today, I'm smiling wryly, for I'm sitting at the dining room table where the final piéce de résistance hangs over my head as I type on my laptop.

For you see, before we cleared everything out of our dream home, this beautiful woman, our buyer, gave me a call.

"Holly, I heard that the dining room light is very special to you. Why don't you just go ahead and take it with you? I have other plans for that room anyway. It's OK."

And now my dining room light is a gift that has been given to me twice. If I ever doubt God's love and grace, all I have to do is turn on that soft tiffany light, feel it's light soak down around me, and I'm resting and relaxing in His love all over again.

What If?

MARSHA JORDAN

D ue to complications of a connective tissue disease, without warning I'd been struck blind. Doctors tried treatment after treatment in a race to stop the damage to my eyes before it was too late. After each daily examination, the cornea specialist would hold his hand in front of my face and ask how many fingers I could see. Hope dwindled, as day after day I replied, "None."

As I lay awake in the lonely darkness, I prayed harder than I'd ever prayed before. The last several weeks, I had been living in the middle of my most dreaded nightmare. I felt alone, frustrated, sad, and afraid. All my plans and dreams for the future were hanging by a thin thread that could break at any moment.

The searing pain stabbed at my eyes. It felt as if fire were consuming them. But it wasn't pain that caused my sleeplessness. Worse than the excruciating physical torment was the terrifying darkness and the agonizing over the "what ifs."

What if I accidentally pulled the protective coverings off in my sleep and rubbed my eyes against the pillow?

The doctor had warned me to avoid even a slight touch to my inflamed corneas.

What if I would never regain my sight? What if I couldn't take care of myself? What if I couldn't drive my car and be independent anymore? What if I would never enjoy reading a book, watching a sunset, or—worst of all —gazing into the eyes of my beautiful grandbaby?

During the long, sleepless nights, I fumed in disbelief, "Why is this happening? I *can't* be permanently blinded!" In despair, I cried silently in my heart, questioning God. But I had to hold back the tears because crying irritated my eyes more.

Besides the torturous pain and the devastating fear of not regaining my vision, there was the anxiety over how to pay the medical bills. The cost of one doctor visit was a staggering $800, and I saw the doctor daily for six weeks.

I'd become very protective of my eyes and skittish about anything coming near them. I needed Valium just to be coaxed into the examining chair. When he came toward me with tweezers, I recoiled in terror and practically had to be held down. I soaked the chair with perspiration during each doctor visit and I literally shook with fear at the thought of him touching my eyes. So you can understand my reaction when the surgeon announced that he needed to cut my cornea, lift it, and clean under it. I told him, "I'd rather have my legs amputated!"

They say courage is fear that's said its prayers. I learned that truth by experience. I knew there were many people praying for me, my home church as well as churches across the country and even around the globe. I, too, prayed fervently. I begged God, not only for healing of my eyes, but for strength to endure whatever happened. I had to put my trust in Him because He was in control, and He was the only one who could help me.

While lying awake one night, I clicked on the TV. An all-night station played gentle music as a man read soothing Bible passages. It comforted and calmed me, so I began looking forward to listening every night. I was awake anyway, and it helped the hours pass more quickly.

Like a fountain of fresh water, God's Word, combined with the soothing music, rinsed away my anxiety and worries and replaced them with peace. I was reminded of the words of Jesus: "Peace I leave with you; my peace I give to you. . . . Do not let your hearts be troubled and do not be afraid" (John 14:27). At last, I was able to say, "Whatever You want, God."

I gave my fears to God and determined to believe in His love for me. I knew He would keep His hand on me, no matter what happened. And I knew He wanted only what was best for me, so why should I fear? If He chose to heal me, I would be unspeakably grateful. If He chose not to, I would remember that He had a reason for that, too. No matter what, with His help, I could go on with my life and use it for Him.

The surgery went well; in time my eyes healed, and my world grew brighter. The pain subsided, and the blackness gradually became a white fog. It was a long road to recovery, but I defied all odds. Slowly the fog grew clearer. After the ordeal, my doctor confided that he hadn't believed I would ever see again. He told me it was a miracle, but I already knew that.

Actually, God gave me two miracles. He healed my eyes, restoring my sight when doctors believed it was hopeless. And, like a plant bursting forth from a dead seed, faith, hope, and trust had blossomed from my fear. Perhaps that was an even greater miracle.

On to Africa!

ELIZABETH RAINES
AS TOLD TO MELODY RAIN

T he plane landed in Sao Paulo, Brazil, after passing over rows and rows of tiny stucco structures. On the ground I was greeted by floral gardens, brown faces, unruly traffic, whiffs of bakery goods and spices, and a commotion of activity typical of large Latin American cities.

To this bustling megalopolis of 22 million inhabitants, where magnificent high rises and rundown shacks exist side by side, I had come to assist in a classroom lecturing program at the University of Sao Paulo. The schedule for the week included much activity. My part in the training program was to lecture for up to eight hours. The rest of the time I was to work individually with Brazilian educators.

Ready for this pace after a long illness, I quickly got in step with my Latin friends, loving and reveling in every moment of liveliness and usefulness. For a number of years I had suffered from chronic fatigue syndrome (CFS), a debilitating virus which held my body in check and confined me to four bedroom walls. Every effort I made toward healing had failed to rally my body. It became difficult, therefore, to believe that I would see bright days again when the pull of illness and the glum statistics (currently less than a 25 percent recovery rate) urged me in the opposite direction of doubt and discouragement. I despaired of ever again seeing healthy days.

Though I was never tempted to quit seeking health, I wrestled often with hopelessness, the kind that haunts you and, even when you shoo it away, returns. Finally I met a doctor who promised me she could get me well. It took a lot of work, but gradually my health program and prayers paid off and the CFS left my body.

"You have a depth of understanding of people and complex subjects," Marcos, my Brazilian host, commented. "You have so much to offer us!"

I sensed this was true. There had been much waiting, enduring, and hoping while my skills and abilities were put on hold. How I longed to travel, teach, and be a full participator in life. Now my calendar was brimming with productive opportunities. Life was good—hard earned, but the sweeter for it! Surely heaven had opened to me.

The first days in Sao Paulo were filled with a constant hum of activity. The demands pushed my adrenalin levels high as I noticed how well my body was responding under pressure. At dinner one evening I shared with my fellow workers the triumph I was experiencing over my long illness. Little did I know the challenges to that accomplishment that lay ahead.

The next morning complimentary warm sweet cakes, fresh papaya, pineapple, and steaming Brazilian coffee awaited the guests in the hotel dining room. But I was not tempted. I awoke with a flu-like sensation. In the background I could hear people in the corridor of the large hotel. My coworkers were getting ready for their part in the day ahead. I was scheduled to instruct my new Brazilian friends on overcoming challenges. I wanted to bounce out of bed, don my most attractive suit, heels, and jewelry, but I had been taken under siege. The harder I tried to rouse myself, the more confused I became. I felt like I was playing an old record.

At last my traveling companion entered the sleeping area to wake me. "Time to rise and shine." Instead of being greeted with a gleeful traveler, my friend knew I was ill . . . very ill.

Hours later I was told that I had yellow fever, a life-threatening parasitic disease resulting from an infected mosquito bite. The infection rate of yellow fever had dropped worldwide in recent years, yet, even with the best medical attention, a sizeable percentage of those who contract this disease die within the first four to nine days. For those who survive the invader, a natural immunity develops which will prevent a recurrence of yellow fever.

It was imperative that I get home. I needed proper medical attention from my own doctor who understood my particular vulnerabilities. I called Dr. Allen. "Look in the box I sent you," she said.

I glanced at the package I had received the day before. I had ordered calcium to help me sleep and had assumed the box had nothing else in it. Looking closer, I saw a one-ounce bottle labeled "Yellow Fever."

"I received a sample of yellow fever medication before your last order, and I decided to send it along. It's very strong. Get on it right away," she insisted.

During the twenty-hour flight to the United States I remained dizzy and feverish. At home I continued to lapse in and out of sultry periods of sleep. While awake I took dose after dose of the medication, feeling that each time I did it was helping me regain my strength. Through the cool nights I slept uncovered, my body temperature keeping me well overheated. My back ached, spasms and pain tormenting me. My head had a dull throb as if a large, heavy object were leaning against it. The parasites seemed like tiny but strong aliens, more powerful than I, pummeling away at my body.

My hopes plummeted. Somehow I had felt that once illness was conquered my path would be smooth. But I was forgetting that I live in a real world of steady inclines. Once well, a tiny insect had stolen my strength, imperiled my life, and battled my resolve. Like a woodpecker carving away at a tree, my confidence was being whittled away until, once again, I wearied that life would never be free of the adversity of sickness.

Yellow fever was a setback, not a pronouncement that I would always be sick, I reminded myself. I kept appealing to God, a habit I had learned while struggling with CFS. And as I kept calling on God, my fever began to go down. Then one day, weeks later, I took a book and headed to my hammock to read under the warm sun, my body welcoming the outing. Several months later I was beginning to return to the routine of living. The invader was conquered.

I was reminded through this experience that even if I look the same monstrous ordeal in the eyes over and over and it whispers to me, "You'll never make it through this time," I can recall when my doctor unexpectedly received a remedy and felt the inclination to include the yellow fever medicine with my order, even before she knew I needed it.

It's been almost ten years since I visited Brazil. Since that time my health has not diminished; in fact it has improved, as I have taught in France, Germany, Poland, Bulgaria, and other parts of the world. Next trip? Why not Africa? I'm immune to yellow fever now!

A NOTE FROM THE EDITORS

This original book was created by the Books and Inspirational Media Division of Guideposts, the world's leading inspirational publisher. Founded in 1945 by Dr. Norman Vincent Peale and his wife, Ruth Stafford Peale, Guideposts helps people from all walks of life achieve their maximum personal and spiritual potential. Guideposts is committed to communicating positive, faith-filled principles for people everywhere to use in successful daily living.

Our publications include award-winning magazines like *Guideposts, Angels on Earth, Sweet 16,* and *Positive Thinking,* best-selling books, and outreach services that demontrate what can happen when faith and positive thinking are applied to day-to-day life.

For more information, visit us online at www.guideposts.org, call (800) 431-2344, or write Guideposts, 39 Seminary Hill Road, Carmel, New York 10512.